The Ethics of Global Business

Foundations of Business Ethics

Series editors: W. Michael Hoffman and Robert E. Frederick

Written by an assembly of the most distinguished figures in business ethics, the Foundations of Business Ethics series aims to explain and assess the fundamental issues that motivate interest in each of the main subjects of contemporary research. In addition to a general introduction to business ethics, individual volumes cover key ethical issues in management, marketing, finance, accounting, and computing. The books, which are complementary yet complete in themselves, allow instructors maximum flexibility in the design and presentation of course materials without sacrificing either depth of coverage or the discipline-based focus of many business courses. The volumes can be used separately or in combination with anthologies and case studies, depending on the needs and interests of the instructors and students.

The Ethics of Global Business

Denis G. Arnold

WILEY Blackwell

Registered Office(s)
John Wiley & Sons, Inc., 111 River Street, Hoboken, NJ 07030, USA
John Wiley & Sons Ltd, The Atrium, Southern Gate, Chichester, West Sussex, PO19 8SQ, UK

For details of our global editorial offices, customer services, and more information about Wiley products visit us at www.wiley.com.

Wiley also publishes its books in a variety of electronic formats and by print-on-demand. Some content that appears in standard print versions of this book may not be available in other formats.

Library of Congress Cataloging-in-Publication Data applied for
Paperback ISBN 9781405134781

Cover Design: Wiley
Cover Image: © catastrophe_OL/Shutterstock

Set in 10.5/12.5pt Minion Pro by Straive, Pondicherry, India
Printed and bound by CPI Group (UK) Ltd, Croydon, CR0 4YY

C9781405134781_300123

Contents

Chapter One

Ethics and Transnational Companies

Companies confront challenges to their legitimacy based on activities such as human rights violations, bribery, the exploitation of impoverished workers and consumers, and negative environmental externalities. Typically such cases involve publicly held companies, based in industrialized "home" nations, operating in a developing "host" nations with limited institutional resources for regulating and policing the practices of corporations and their contractors. Critical attention has also been paid to the social and environmental practices of companies based in advanced developing nations, such as Russia or China, operating in Africa and other less-developed regions. The prevalence of these cases is one indication of the fact that we live and work in an era of economic globalization. While trade among nations has been an important feature of the global economy for centuries, there has been a rapid increase in international trade since 1990. The substantial increase in foreign direct investment (FDI) is one indicator of the steadily growing economic and political influence of corporations operating internationally.

Transnational companies (TNCs) operate in a multitude of political juris-dictions and so are subject to a multitude of legal frameworks. Laws regarding such matters as the treatment of customers, the treatment of employees, and environmental protection vary significantly in different host nations. In the case of developing economies, consumer protection, worker safety, and environmental safeguards are often poorly developed. Even when robust laws exist in developing nations, the law enforcement and judicial apparatus necessary to ensure compliance is often weak or corrupt. TNCs operating in such nations are often free to determine for themselves whether or not they will adhere to host nation laws.

FDI can improve social welfare in developing nations through technology transfer, job creation, and economic growth. However, critics challenge the moral

The Ethics of Global Business, First Edition. Denis G. Arnold.

legitimacy of many companies operating in developing nations. Corporate moral legitimacy concerns the evaluation of corporate practices and outcomes from the perspective of diverse stakeholders via the application of moral or ethical norms (Suchman 1995). TNCs confront legitimacy concerns grounded in the perception that they violate basic ethical norms, especially with regard to their relationships with and impacts on base of the pyramid populations. Nongovernmental organizations (NGOs) charge companies with environmental degradation, disregard for the welfare of home-nation employees, and the illegitimate exploitation of offshore factory workers. They argue that when companies move into developing nations they often cause more harm than good for workers, pollute local environments, and illegitimately exploit the natural resources of host nations. For example, NGO and media reports criticize Apple's labor practices in China, Walmart's proactive corruption strategies in Mexico, Disney's use of child labor in supplier factories, China Non-Ferrous Metals Mining Corporation's human rights record in Zambia, and Goldcorp's human rights record in its mining operations in Guatemala, to name only a few examples.

Underlying such allegations are *empirical* claims about the impact of company activities and *normative* claims about how companies should conduct themselves in the global marketplace. The truth of a particular empirical claim about the actions of companies can be properly assessed only when the relevant facts are known and understood. Normative claims are explicitly ethical claims about whether or not the actions of companies are consistent with particular conceptions of right action or justice. Conceptions of right action and justice are the domain of ethics. This book is concerned with the ethical norms that should guide the behavior of companies in their global operations, but the arguments deployed take into account many of the empirical dimensions that are most salient to assessing business practices.

This chapter describes modern TNCs and explains why companies and their leaders are properly regarded as responsible for company policies and practices. We then turn our attention to a theory of the moral legitimacy of TNCs. In Chapter 2, a cosmopolitan perspective on international business ethics is defended. First, the claim that corporations are properly understood as agents of justice is explained and defended. Second, two domains of normative legitimacy regarding international business are distinguished. It is argued that the moral legitimacy of organizations is not persuasively accounted for by a Habermasian deliberative democracy perspective. Third, it is argued that proponents of a Rawlsian political perspective on corporate obligations regarding global justice are mistaken. Taken together, these two sections show that the "political" account of corporate social responsibility (CSR) that has proven influential among some business ethics and CSR scholars in recent years cannot provide an adequate theory of international business ethics. An alternative, "ethical" conception of CSR is then defended utilizing a cosmopolitan human rights perspective.

In Chapter 3, I defend an account of human rights cosmopolitanism. It is argued that human rights are claim rights against parties with whom one stands in a relationship. I argue that human rights are ultimately grounded in human agency or the capacity of persons to govern themselves and that the human rights that TNCs and other business enterprises have duties to protect and respect are basic rather than aspirational. In chapter 4, I provide a critical analysis of recent United Nations (UN) initiatives on business and human rights. It is argued that the UN Draft Norms initiative is properly regarded as an example of the "dark side" of human rights. It is then argued that the more recent UN tripartite framework on human rights developed by the UN Secretary-General's Special Representative for Business and Human Rights, and subsequently approved by the UN Human Rights Council, and implemented by the Organisation for Economic Co-operation and Development (OECD) and the International Finance Committee (IFC), has conceptual and analytic weaknesses. It is argued that the tripartite framework cannot be properly regarded as having a merely strategic foundation, but must be regarded as having an ethical foundation grounded in respect for basic human rights. Once this has been provided, the coherence of the tripartite framework is improved. In Chapter 5, the cosmopolitan human rights theory articulated in chapters 2–4 is defended against criticisms.

In chapter 6, this human rights framework is extended to working conditions in global supply chains. This chapter defends minimum standards for factory workers regarding the disclosure of risks and health and safety conditions and provides an analysis of wage exploitation in developing nations.

The next two chapters provide an ethical analyses of base of the pyramid (BoP) strategies. Proponents of BoP strategies argue that TNCs can reap enhanced profitability by targeting the four billion people living at the base of the economic pyramid as consumers while providing the poor with valuable goods or services. In Chapter 7, my concern is specifically with that portion of the BoP comprised of the 2.6 billion people living in moderate and extreme (MEP) poverty or less than $2 a day. It is argued that MEP populations are both cognitively and socially vulnerable, rendering them susceptible to harmful exploitation. An empowerment theory of morally legitimate BoP business ventures is defended and a multi-stage opportunity assessment process is described that allows TNC managers to determine when BoP ventures should be pursued and when they should be abandoned. This analysis is then used to criticize instrumental CSR and to defend ethical CSR. In Chapter 8, it is argued that businesses that engage in BoP activities with the ostensible goal of benefitting BoP populations may paradoxically harm BoP populations by degrading the natural environments upon that sustain BoP populations. This chapter provides a conceptual framework for understanding the environmental impacts that firm products, services, and operations can have on the poor. A pragmatic solution aimed at resolving this apparent paradox is then provided.

Transnational Companies

A variety of types and sizes of companies operate internationally. Small or medium sized firms may have supply chains that extend across national boundaries or may service foreign customers, but are based in one nation. Larger organizations that have operations and employees in many nations are the primary subject of analysis in this work. Bartlett and Ghoshal (2002) provide a conceptual framework for understanding the different types of organizational structures of large firms operating in an international context. In recent history, they argue, there have been three main types of organizational structures. First, there are multinational companies characterized by a decentralized governance structure with self-sufficient companies operating in host nations. The strategy of multinational companies is based on sensitivity and *responsiveness* to national contexts, and knowledge acquired and retained within national units. Second, there are global companies that are characterized by the centralized governance of a parent company operating from a home nation. The strategy of global companies is characterized by the *efficient* deployment of a uniform strategy in host-nations, and knowledge acquired and retained by the center. Finally, there are international companies that are characterized by a combination of centralized and decentralized core competencies. International companies utilize a strategy of *leveraging* parent company competencies grounded in knowledge acquired centrally and distributed overseas (Bartlett and Ghoshal 2002, pp. 16–18).[1]

Bartlett and Ghoshal argue that in order for modern TNCs to adapt to a global marketplace and remain competitive, they need to be responsive to national contexts, efficient in their global operations, and capable of leveraging parent company competencies. That is, they argue that companies need to adapt key attributes from each of the three types of companies operating globally in order to be economically successful. In this work, the term "transnational companies" will be utilized more broadly to encompass multinational companies, global companies, and international companies, as well as the model of TNCs that Ghoshal and Bartlett advise general managers to adapt. Each type of company is transnational in the sense that the scope of company operations, customer base, or supply chains extend across national boundaries and often into regulatory and governance gaps. While characteristics described by Ghoshal and Bartlett are important for understanding the differences between the varieties of companies operating internationally, and the strategic advantages and disadvantages of each variety, the differences are insignificant for the purpose of justifying the ethical norms that should inform business practices.

Shareholder Primacy

Bartlett and Ghoshal's typology of companies is ostensibly amoral, making no normative claims about the obligations of TNCs operating across national boundaries. Elsewhere, however, Ghoshal chastises business school faculty for teaching bad theories about the normative obligations of managers to generations of business school students. In particular, he argues that "by propagating ideologically inspired amoral theories, business schools have actively freed their students from any sense of moral responsibility" (Ghoshal 2005, p. 76). He identifies the shareholder primacy ideology, grounded in unrealistic and unfounded assumptions, as a leading example of a bad theory, which has contributed to the bad practices of managers that result in harm to a variety of stakeholders. While Bartlett and Ghoshal do not advocate shareholder primacy in their analysis of international business, their general silence on the role of ethics in international business is illustrative of much mainstream work in the field, which is primarily the domain of descriptive and empirical social science research. International business scholars have noted the need for greater integration of business ethics and international business (Doh et al. 2010). John Dunning, one of the founders of the field of international business, maintains that in the global marketplace, "human dignity and human rights" are "absolute and universal virtues" that must be recognized and protected by corporations (Dunning 2001). However, there remains little agreement regarding the theoretical framework that should guide international businesses operating in the diverse nations and cultures in which TNCs and their subsidiaries operate.

What ethical norms should guide TNCs in their global operations? This straightforward question generates lively debate among scholars, business leaders, and critics of business alike. The conventional Anglo-American story regarding the normative obligations of corporate managers holds that it is the obligation of managers to maximize profits for shareholders (or private equity holders) while adhering to the law. Sometimes it is added that corporations should also avoid deception, although this is typically stipulated as an aside and not explained or defended by proponents of the "shareholder primacy" perspective (Stout 2012). This view is sometimes summarized by the popular expression that "the business of business is business." Proponents of this view typically emphasize the importance of protecting property rights and the positive impact corporations have on social utility. They argue that managers who expend corporate resources on activities that are not focused on corporate profits are, in effect, undemocratically redistributing investor resources. They also endorse the idea that managers are agents of shareholders who must always act on behalf of shareholder interests. Defenders of this view typically adhere to broadly libertarian beliefs regarding markets emphasizing minimal regulations, private property rights, freedom, especially the freedom to enter into contracts, weak labor protections, and free trade among nations. This nexus of values is, for example, the editorial position of *The Economist*, a magazine with an influential global readership. It is also a position influential among many economists, especially those from the Chicago School of economics, as well as business school faculty influenced by such economists.

This view of the normative function of joint-stock companies may be summarized as follows. First, in democratic nations, citizens determine the rules that govern private property, contracts, and the regulation of markets via their elected and appointed representatives. The courts impartially adjudicate disputes based on precedent and foundational charters or constitutions. Second, in order to reduce transaction costs, citizens facilitate the creation of publicly held corporations that allow for the pooling of investments in business ventures with investor liability limited to the loss of the investment. Third, to efficiently manage the organization shareholders, or private equity investors, utilize boards of directors to retain executives to act as their agents. Fourth, the executives implicitly agree to follow the laws determined by the democratic process, thereby garnering moral legitimacy grounded in respect for a democratic system of government. Fifth, an economic system in which businesses maximize profits for investors within a democratically determined regulatory framework that gives priority to property rights, freedom of contracts, and competitive markets will maximize overall utility measured in monetary terms, at least in comparison to alternative political-economic systems.

The ideological bedfellow of the shareholder primacy view is the instrumental theory of corporate responsibility. Instrumental, or economic, corporate social responsibility holds that corporations should engage in pro-social or ethical conduct only when doing so will improve the return on investment of the financiers of the organization (Gond et al. 2009; McWilliams and Siegel 2001; McWilliams et al. 2006). The term "instrumental" CSR is more appropriate than the term "economic" CSR because it better reflects the idea that the exclusive duty or obligation of managers is to promote shareholder, or financier, wealth, regardless of other ethical considerations. In this sense, pro-social behavior is of instrumental value to shareholders or financiers. On the other hand, the term "economic" refers to a much broader domain of concern and might include, for example, considerations regarding public welfare beyond the narrow interests of shareholders or financiers. According to the instrumental view, the only legitimate role of managers regarding ethical or prosocial behavior is to engage in ongoing cost-benefit analysis that balances the claims and expectations of various stakeholders (both internal and external) against firm profitability. Meeting increased stakeholder expectations will sometimes result in greater demand and improved revenues.

According to the instrumental position regarding corporate responsibilities, in such cases the additional cost is justified because of increased revenues. However, ethical or pro-social behaviors that do not increase revenues are not justified and should not be undertaken. Gond et al. (2009) argue that that the logic of this position is consistent with the institutional logic of the Italian mafia, which has a similar focus on extreme profits and the exploitation of governance gaps.

This theoretical framework is surprisingly problematic given its prominence in public discourse and scholarship about business in the United States (Ghoshal 2005; Jones and Felps 2013). One might think that a view that was defended by influential scholars in finance and economics, as well as many corporate leaders and politicians, would have a firm grounding in a well-developed theory of the legitimacy of corporate practices in a global economic system, but this is not the case. Consider just three of the difficulties with this position: faulty assumptions regarding institutional frameworks, the political influence of corporations and other business interests that the ideology ignores, and the lack of democratic governments in many nations in which corporations conduct business that make the ideology largely inapplicable in many nations in which TNCs operate.

Faulty Assumptions Regarding Institutional Frameworks

The shareholder primacy ideology is grounded in a faulty interpretation of corporate law. Legal scholar Lynn Stout points out that, contrary to the shareholder primacy ideology, corporate law in the United States gives directors and executives wide discretion with regard to corporate objectives via the business judgment rule (Stout 2012). In practice, this entails that managers have the legal right to take into account the actions of their companies on other stakeholders and on society in general. Pressure from Wall Street analysts, major investors, and poorly designed executive incentive structures can encourage a myopic focus on short term stock performance and disregard for the interests of employees or customers, but this is not a legal requirement and many US companies are managed in a way that balances the interests of multiple stakeholders (for further discussion of the US legal context for corporations, see Orts (2013)).

In the United Kingdom, the revised Companies Act of 2006 requires that directors take into account the interest's of the company's employees, "the impact of the company's operations on the community and the environment," the need to maintain "a reputation for high standards of business conduct," and the need to act fairly.[2] More generally, 15 of 27 members states of the European Union have national policy frameworks for promoting corporate social responsibility. The European Commission, the executive governing body of the European Union, has recommended that all member states implement such frameworks.[3] The India Companies Act of 2013 mandates that large firms operating in India contribute 2% of net profits to CSR initiatives and monitor and report on their initiatives.[4]

The shareholder primacy view is also parochial in the context of a global marketplace in its assumption that companies are based in liberal market economies, such as the United States, while ignoring the varieties of capitalism that exist in the world. Liberal market economies (e.g. the United States, Britain, Canada, Australia, Ireland, and New Zealand) are characterized by competitive markets in which access to capital is linked to current market performance and labor markets are fluid because the institutional arrangements to provide job security are limited (Hall and Soskice 2001, pp. 8–19; Williamson 1985). Coordinated market economies (e.g. Germany, Japan, Switzerland, Sweden, Norway, and Austria) rely significantly on nonmarket forms of coordination via networks and collaborative relationships. In these markets, access to capital is independent of recent stock performance and institutional structures within the economy are designed to result in long-term employment relationships.

Institutional arrangements in coordinated economies typically require companies to take into account the interests of other stakeholders and society in general in their policies and practices. For example, in Germany, codetermination laws ensure that employees constitute one-half of the membership of the boards of directors of most companies with more than 2000 employees, and one-third of the members of the boards of directors of most companies between 500 and 2000 employees (as well as many stock companies with employees fewer than 499 employees). Codetermination laws give employees significant controlling influence over companies in the interest of protecting employee welfare (Fauver and Fuerst 2006). Additional varieties of capitalism exist in other nations or regions.[5] For example, China's economy is characterized by tight central coordination and the strategic use of state-owned enterprises.

Democratic Legitimacy

The ideal of representative democracy that is an essential feature of the shareholder primacy view, one where citizens determine the rules of the game and companies adhere to those rules while maximizing shareholder wealth, is incompatible with the reality of modern interest group politics. One way of understanding democracy is in terms of plural interest groups competing for political influence. In this view, the democratic process is comprised of shifting coalitions of interests groups that reflect the interests of their members. The disproportionately influential role that corporations and their surrogates play in shaping the rules of the game is largely ignored by proponents of the shareholder primacy view. In the United States, for example, polls consistently find that a large majority of Americans believe that corporations exert too much political influence.[6] In his classic book on the topic of corporate political influence, *Politics and Markets*, Charles Lindblom argues that corporations in democracies exert power over governments in two primary ways (Lindblom 1977; see also Epstein 1969 and Wilson 1981). First, corporations and their surrogates exert ideological power by shaping public preferences. Second, corporations exert political power through political action committees and paid lobbyists.[7] Lindblom's conclusions are well supported by social science data compiled in the United States and Great Britain (Mitchell 1997). A survey of the empirical data on this subject by political scientist Neil Mitchell found that the preponderance of evidence supports the conclusion that a disproportionate expenditure of resources by business interests has resulted in special benefits for corporations. A more recent meta-analysis of research on corporate political activity corroborates Mitchell's conclusions and finds that firms that expend more on corporate political activity financially outperform firms that expend less (Lux et al. 2011).

Proponents of shareholder primacy have yet to provide a theory of corporate political activity that situates corporate power in democratic theory and provides an account of legitimate corporate political activity. It is difficult to see how such a theory could justify an advocacy role for corporations in party politics above and beyond the rights enjoyed by individual employees, shareholders, and customers as citizens, even if corporations enjoy other certain rights. But in a global business environment this is just one challenge with respect to democracy confronting proponents of the shareholder primacy theory of the firm. A second, and more fundamental problem, is the absence of democracy in many environments in which TNCs operate.

Many of the nations in which TNCs conduct business lack important democratic institutions such as equal voting rights, multiple political parties, democratic elections, politically neutral militaries, and an independent judiciary. According to Freedom House, 57.4% of the world's sovereign states and colonial units—home to 57% of the world's population—lack civil or political freedom (Freedom House 2020). Forty percent of nations including China, Russia, and Nigeria are not electoral democracies. The shareholder primacy view presumes the existence of electoral democracies, and presumably civil and political rights that facilitate political speech and activity, so that citizens can regulate business activity. The shareholder primacy view is inapplicable in other political contexts. However, international business is conducted in all nations, and a theory of the firm that cannot provide guidance to companies operating in unfree or partially free nations is inapplicable for transnational companies operating in a global economy and can provide no guidance to firms operating primarily in nations that are not democratically governed.

Regulatory and Governance Gaps

In nondemocratic nations, as well as in many electoral democracies, there are regulatory and governance gaps pertaining to business operations. A regulatory gap refers to a substantive lack of regulation regarding some type of business activity. In this context, the gaps we are concerned with are those that permit harm to human welfare (e.g. gaps in the protection of internationally recognized labor rights, or in environmental laws that protect water and air quality, or in financial regulations preventing usurious loans). Such gaps are filled by regulations that better protect citizens from exploitation and the degradation of the environments in which they live. Many developing nation have such governance gaps that companies have historically utilized to advance profit maximization.

A governance gap refers to institutional failures to enforce existing regulations regarding any type of business activity. This may be the result of political turmoil, weak or corrupt governments, or a lack of resources necessary to police and enforce existing regulations. Governance gaps are present in many developing nations and in Russia and former Soviet bloc nations. Governance gaps often prevent the enforcement of regulations intended to protect citizens from physical harm or deprivation and the degradation of the natural environments in which citizens live and upon which they depend upon for their livelihood.

TNCs exploit governance gaps when they or their suppliers violate local laws in their business operations with the knowledge that local authorities are unable or unwilling to adequately enforce existing regulations. A failure to adhere to host nation laws and regulations can result in costs savings, faster turn-around time for production orders, increased access to markets, or greater sales. Violation of the law may be routine and incorporated into the business strategy of a TNC, or it might be the decision of one or more subsidiaries of a multinational company with a decentralized and nationally self-sufficient organizational structure, or it may be undertaken by suppliers who are not carefully monitored by a company.

It is difficult to assess how widespread the practice of violating host nation laws may be among TNCs, their subsidiaries, and suppliers. Recently, the United States Securities and Exchange Commission stepped up enforcement of the US Foreign Corrupt Practices Act. Bribery is typically illegal in the host-nations where it takes place but governance gaps result in lax enforcement by authorities. Among the 60 companies that the US Securities and Exchange Commission has taken enforcement actions against recently for corruption are US-based General Electric for corruption in Iraq; Eli Lily for corruption in Russia, Brazil, China, and Poland; Pfizer for corruption in Bulgaria, China, Croatia, the Czech Republic, Kazakhstan, Russia, and Serbia;

Johnson & Johnson for corruption in Poland, Romania and Iraq; IBM for corruption in China, KBR and its former parent Halliburton for corruption in Nigeria; London-based Diageo for corruption in India and Thailand; French-based Alcatel-Lucent for corruption in Costa Rica; and the German company Siemens for corruption in Indonesia. Corruption and bribery are unique in that the violation of host-nation laws also violates US law (as well as the 2010 UK Bribery Act) providing an incentive for companies to maintain an active compliance and corruption prevention program. The violation of labor and environmental laws in host nations do not normally also violate US, UK, or EU laws and as result companies have less incentive for compliance with these laws.

The logic of the shareholder primacy perspective and instrumental CSR encourages the exploitation of regulatory and governance gaps. First, governance and regulatory gaps often exist in nondemocratic nations where the shareholder primacy ideology is inapplicable. Second, in developing nations that are also democracies, but with weak governance institutions, the relentless pursuit of profit advocated by the shareholder ideology implicitly advocates illegal activity when such activity is profitable and governments are unable to enforce existing regulations. Proponents of the shareholder primacy ideology and instrumental CSR have been conspicuously silent on the question of what obligations TNCs have when, for example, labor and environmental laws go unenforced in developing nations.

Conclusion

Companies operating internationally are properly held accountable for corporate policies and practices in the host nations in which they operate. The shareholder primacy ideology and its logical extension, instrumental CSR, are inadequate theoretical frameworks for assessing and guiding the behavior of TNCs. The remainder of this book is focused on the development of a theoretical framework that is applicable in democratic as well as nondemocratic contexts, that is consistent with emerging global standards regarding corporate responsibilities, and that acknowledges the unique challenges of companies operating in nations with regulatory and governance gaps.

Notes

1. Significantly, many of the companies Bartlett and Ghoshal utilized as research subjects in order to generate this framework have failed or had to sell-off or shut down traditional business units because they could not adapt a successful global strategy.
2. United Kingdom, Companies Act 2006, 172(1).

3. European Commission (2011).
4. The India Companies Act of 2013 (Chap. IX, Sec. 135).
5. Mediterranean economies (e.g. France, Italy, Spain, Portugal, Greece, Turkey) share in common large agrarian sectors, and like coordinated market economies, they enjoy certain capacities for nonmarket coordination of corporate finance. However, they share more liberal employment relationships with liberal market economies (Hall and Soskice 2001).
6. Business Week/Harris Poll (2000), Hart Research Associates (2010), and Harris Poll (2012).
7. Lindblom also develops a third argument regarding corporate power. This argument, frequently referred to as the structural dependence thesis, holds that corporations exert structural power by virtue of their ability to affect voters' assessment of government. This, in turn, leads governments to prefer policies that are advantageous to business. This argument is not discussed below, primarily because it does not appear to be well supported by empirical data.

Chapter Two

Global Justice and International Business

My aim in this chapter is to address the question of what theoretical framework is best suited for determining the obligations transnational corporations and other business organizations have to those individuals with whom they interact in their global operations. My argument is developed in four parts. First, the claim that corporations are properly understood as agents of justice is explained and defended. Second, two domains of normative legitimacy regarding international business are distinguished. It is argued that the moral legitimacy of organizations is not persuasively accounted for by the Habermasian deliberative democracy perspective that has been defended by management scholars (Scherer and Palazzo 2007). Third, it is argued that proponents of a Rawlsian political perspective on corporate obligations regarding global justice are mistaken. The upshot of these two sections is that the political account of corporate social responsibility (CSR) that has proven influential among some scholars in recent years cannot provide an adequate theoretical account of the obligations of corporations in the international arena. In the fourth part of the article, an alternative ethical perspective on CSR that utilizes a cosmopolitan human rights perspective is introduced. This cosmopolitan perspective will be elaborated and defended in subsequent chapters.

Agents of Global Justice

Global justice is a topic of broad concern and one of the most lively and dynamic areas of contemporary scholarship in political philosophy. Among the central concerns of global justice scholars are the just distribution of global resources and the legitimacy of the global institutional order in light

The Ethics of Global Business, First Edition. Denis G. Arnold.
© 2023 John Wiley & Sons Ltd. Published 2023 by John Wiley & Sons Ltd.

of global poverty. Much of the debate regarding global justice concerns just relations among states (or "peoples" in the idiosyncratic language of Rawls) (Rawls 1999) individual responsibility for the global institutional order (Pogge 2002b, 2005; Reitberger 2008; Young 2004, 2006), and the legitimacy of global governance institutions (e.g., the World Bank, International Monetary Fund, and the United Nations) (Buchanan and Keohane 2006; Keohane 2011). To the extent that they are discussed at all, corporations are typically discussed as subjects of control by the basic institutional structures of nations.

There are no doubt many reasonable explanations for this relative lack of interest in corporations by global justice scholars, but let us focus on two of these. First, part of the explanation for this relative lack of attention to these important global actors is sociological. While significant philosophical contributions to the literature on global justice have been made by scholars working in moral philosophy, the literature on global justice is most often the domain of political philosophers (including those trained in political science or government departments) and philosophers of international law. Through training and disciplinary focus, these scholars are inclined to focus on political systems, governmental institutions, and legal frameworks, rather than business enterprises. The significant international business ethics literature that initially emerged in the 1990s has had little impact on developments in the global justice literature and tends to be ignored by these scholars.[1]

The second reason involves differences in judgment regarding the role of corporations and other business enterprises in contributing to global justice and is well illustrated by the debate between Onora O'Neill (2001) and David Held (2002). O'Neill argues that corporations should be understood as agents of global justice. By "agents," O'Neill means only that they act on behalf of justice and not the more substantive claim that TNCs are genuine moral agents. Corporations, she argues, operate as secondary agents of justice in powerful nation states, but may operate as the primary agent of justice in weak or failed states. As O'Neill acknowledges, this is not a novel claim either from the perspective of theorists or from the perspective of corporate managers (2001, p. 200). Nonetheless, her claim met with resistance from Held. While acknowledging that important differences exist between corporations with regard to their attitudes toward global justice, Held argues that O'Neill is mistaken to focus attention on corporations rather than regional and global regulatory regimes. He argues that substantially different regulatory environments in different nations will lead corporations to seek out the least burdensome regulatory environments in order to remain competitive, resulting in a classic "race to the bottom" scenario (Held 2002, p. 71). To avoid this undesirable outcome, Held recommends a two-pronged solution. First, "entrenchment of revised rules, codes and procedures ... in the articles of association and terms of reference of economics organizations and trading agencies" (Held 2002, pp. 72–73).[2] Second, the adaptation of cosmopolitan principles by regional and global institutions.

Significantly, the debate between O'Neill and Held did not spark new lines of research among global justice scholars regarding the role that corporations should play in the moral division of labor regarding justice. Indeed, this debate effectively died off after Held's rejoinder suggesting that global justice theorists who have reflected on these issues are sympathetic to Held's position. If most global justice theorists maintain something like Held's view that the role of corporations in global justice is a problem of global regulation and not a management issue, then it is not surprising that we have not seen more attention paid to corporations and other business enterprises in the global justice literature.

While there is a place for some of Held's recommended solutions, there are reasons familiar to scholars of international business and business ethics for thinking that he is mistaken to dismiss the roles of corporations in promoting global justice. First, Held's position is grounded in empirical claims about corporate behavior for which he provides no evidence. A lack of attention to empirical studies regarding the beneficial and harmful impacts of various features of contemporary globalization is a deficiency of philosophical scholarship on global justice in general (Blake 2012). Corporations and other business enterprises can benefit or harm diverse global populations in a variety of direct and indirect ways. For example, corporations have direct, positive impacts on the economies of developing nations by transferring technical and managerial knowledge. Firms have indirect, positive impacts via technology spillover and contributions to business infrastructure (Rugman and Doh 2008). Firms have direct or negative impacts as well. For example, direct harm occurs when a corporation's products or labor conditions injure customers or workers. Indirect harm occurs when the general operations of corporations or other business enterprises result in harmful externalities, such as air pollution, water table drainage, or the introduction of carcinogens into local environments.

Second, substantial bodies of scholarship in industrial organization and behavioral business ethics have shown that an instrumental account of practical reasoning, one in which profitability is the only motive managers utilize in making business policy decisions, is an inadequate explanation of firm behavior.[3] Institutional structures, organizations incentives, bounded rationality, ethical values, and stakeholder perceptions of legitimacy can each contribute to the determination of business policy regarding activities impacting the BoP.

Third, global or regional rules and regulations intended to modify the behavior of corporations in weak, unstable, or failed states typically will be ineffectual unless firms conscientiously choose to adhere to those rules and regulations. These nations often lack the regulatory oversight and infrastructure necessary to enforce their own laws, or refrain from using such force because national leaders are fearful that the TNC will move operations elsewhere if local laws are enforced. It is unlikely that new rules or regulations will have the desired outcomes without voluntary adherence on the part of firms. The final reason that Held's position is unpersuasive is that there is no obvious basis for thinking that the idea that corporations can and should act as agents of justice is incompatible with the idea that global regulatory regimes can and should be enhanced to provide additional incentives for firms to promote justice.

Institutional Legitimacy

Legitimacy is a topic that has received considerable attention from political philosophers and management scholars, but the distinct types of moral legitimacy relevant to international business has received less attention than is merited by the subject. The debate between O'Neill and Held is instructive insofar as it highlights a distinction between two different domains of normative legitimacy regarding corporations and other business enterprises operating in the international sphere.[4] First, there is the question of the normative legitimacy of the international institutions and rules that govern international trade and regulate international business activity. Here, questions of legitimacy concern the basis of authority, the procedures by which rules or regulations are determined, the substantive content of those rules, and the legitimate enforcement of those rules. Given our focus on the obligations of corporations and other business enterprises, we won't take up this topic here (for discussion see Buchanan and Keohane 2006; Cohen and Sabin 2006; Keohane 2011). Second, there is the question of the normative legitimacy of the corporation itself, especially with regard to its activities in burdened societies. The general issue of corporate legitimacy has received modest attention from management scholars (Palazzo and Scherer 2006; Suchman 1995). As we saw in Chapter 1, at its most basic, moral legitimacy entails "a positive normative evaluation of the organization and its activities" (Suchman 1995, p. 579).

The global context for business is unique insofar as it involves firms operating in a multiplicity of political contexts and in environments with weak or corrupt institutional frameworks (Arnold 2003b; Matten and Crane 2005; Kobrin 2009). Palazzo and Scherer acknowledge this problem and argue that moral legitimacy cannot depend on universal moral or legal norms since there is no widespread agreement on their legitimacy (Palazzo and Scherer 2006, p. 77). Instead, they argue that moral legitimacy should be conceived of as "deliberative communication" (Palazzo and Scherer 2006, p. 73) and, drawing from Habermas, emphasize the importance of democratic control of the "state-like role of the corporation" (Scherer et al. 2006, p. 515). By "state-like role," the authors have in mind the ability of transnational corporations to act as administrators of rights in their global operations.

There are at three serious difficulties with this deliberative democracy perspective on moral legitimacy of corporations. First, it is not clear what this view entails in practice. Let us call this the *process* objection. Modern transnational corporations may have operations spanning the globe that impact billions of people. Pragmatically, it is not clear how these diverse and conflicting perspectives are to be reflected in corporate governance. Is each individual impacted by corporate operations, products, and services to have an equivalent role in the determination of business policy? How might such a process work? Is the process compatible with the multiple regulatory frameworks under which companies operate? Should the process be the same for publicly traded companies, large private companies, state-owned enterprises, and small- and medium-sized enterprises? Does it matter whether or not the firm is operating in a democratic or non-democratic nation? How can a consultative, deliberative process involving millions or billions of people be made compatible with the pace of innovation, dynamics of shifting competition, and technical expertise that are basic features of a global marketplace? Without a theoretical model of deliberation that takes into account these challenges, it remains unclear how the deliberative model constitutes a coherent account of moral legitimacy. However, such a theoretical model has not yet been provided and, on its face, it is difficult to imagine that one that could address these myriad difficulties could be provided.

Second, at least 4 billion people globally are living at the base of the economic pyramid on less than $9.05/day (including 2.6 billion people living on less than $2.00 a day) (see Chapter 5). It is not clear how these BoP populations can have a role in corporate governance given their impoverishment, vulnerability, and high levels of illiteracy. Let us call this the *voice* objection. BoP populations are most vulnerable to harmfully exploitative products and services that are profitable for corporations and benefit other stakeholders, such as employees and shareholders in both democratic and nondemocratic nations. Given the range of disadvantages faced by BoP populations, it is not clear how their perspectives can be incorporated into a democratic process of global governance in a meaningful way, given the size, power, and sheer number of corporations and other business enterprises involved. In functional representative democracies, the voices of the BoP may be heard through the standard political process; but it seems clear that this not what Palazzo and Scherer have in mind with they argue for deliberative democracy as a basis for establishing the moral legitimacy of corporations. Without the ability to specify a process by which the BoP can be empowered to help determine business policy, the idea that democratic deliberation can provide corporations with moral legitimacy appears unfeasible.

Third, introducing deliberative democracy into corporate governance may have unanticipated, negative outcomes on social welfare. Let us call this *negative consequences* objection. Opening up internal corporate governance to democratic control by external stakeholders of any variety (Scherer et al. 2006, p. 520) can result in a loss of efficiency and productivity, reducing firm competitiveness and limiting the capacity of the firm to create value for society.

Proponents of deliberative democracy as a source of moral legitimacy may be able to respond to process, voice, and consequences objections, but it is also possible that an alternative approach to assessing the role of corporations in promoting global justice can provide a better account of corporate moral legitimacy in the global business arena. Such an account should not be susceptible to the practical and theoretical deficiencies of the political CSR approach. An alternative approach to the question of how firms can gain moral legitimacy in a global context is one that utilizes ethical principles that can be incorporated into corporate business policies and operations. This ethical conception of CSR is different from both political CSR and instrumental CSR (Scherer and Palazzo 2011; Windsor 2006). However, before adapting such an approach, we must determine what theoretical approach to global justice is most viable for establishing ethical principles for international business.

Against Rawls

The recent philosophical literature concerning global justice may be divided into two competing categories. Proponents of the *political* view of justice maintain that a system of global socio-economic justice should be grounded in political systems, rather than in ethical norms (Nagel 2005; Rawls 1999). Democracy, in this view, is essential to the legitimacy of political systems. Advocates of this view maintain that justice should be understood primarily as a political value, rather than a moral value. They see justice as a virtue of sovereign states, one that legitimately extends to the citizens of such a state as a result of the willingness of citizens to honor the laws of the state and defend it against the aggression of other states. *Cosmopolitans* maintain that a system of global socio-economic justice must be grounded in ethical principles such as respect for basic human rights or utilitarian welfare maximization (Caney 2005; Pogge 2002 a, b; Singer 1972; Unger 1996). Cosmopolitans see political institutions as a means to ensure respect for such universal norms. Nation-states that contribute to the violation of basic rights, or merely tolerate the violations of such rights, are problems that must be overcome. Proponents of this view typically call for the creation of institutions that have both the power and legitimate authority to compensate for failed states, stabilize weak states, and coerce successful states into respecting relevant ethical norms.

The political view of global justice is distinct from political CSR. Political CSR has been defined as "an extended model of governance with business firms contributing to global regulation and providing public goods" (Scherer and Palazzo 2011: 17). It is both a description of some types of business activity and normative insofar as it defends a particular conception of the legitimacy of business organizations (Makinen and Kourula 2012; Whelan 2012). As we have seen, Scherer and Palazzo defend a Habermasian deliberative democracy perspective regarding corporate legitimacy but that is only one possible political account of the role of corporations in promoting global justice. A contrasting Rawlsian perspective on corporate duties regarding global justice also merits attention because of the scope and influence of Rawls' conception of justice and because Rawlsian arguments have previously been utilized to assess corporate obligations to the BoP (Hsieh 2004, 2009; Santos and Laczniak 2009). Rawls has also been invoked by political CSR scholars in a way that suggests that a Rawlsian perspective is compatible with a Habermasian perspective (Scherer and Palazzo 2007). For these reasons, it is important to assess whether or not a Rawlsian perspective on global justice can serve as the basis for a theory of international business ethics. Since the Rawlsian perspective is only one possible political perspective on global justice, in the remainder of this section, we will refer to the Rawlsian theory of global justice rather than to the broader category of a political view of global justice. Our focus continues to be on the question of corporate obligations regarding global justice, rather than obligations that may arise for nations or individuals as a result of the global institutional frameworks that emerged in the twentieth century and are increasingly influential in the twenty-first century.[5]

To understand a Rawlsian view of the role of corporations in global justice, it is necessary to understand one of Rawls' reasons for favoring a dualist conception of moral theory. Rawls argues that the basic structure of society ought to be regarded as the first subject of justice, at least on a Kantian contractarian view (Rawls 1996). He characterizes the basic structure as "the way in which the major social institutions fit together into one system and, and how they assign fundamental rights and duties and shape the division of advantages that arise through social cooperation" (Rawls 1996, p. 258). Dualism refers to the claim that "the two practical problems of institutional design and personal conduct require, at the fundamental level, two different kinds of practical principle" (Murphy 1998, p. 254). On Rawls' account, the division of duties is between political institutions and individual persons. One justification given by Rawls for this division has to do with a fair distribution of labor in order to ensure that the demands of justice are met. Rawls thinks this is best accomplished by:

> an institutional division of labor between the basic structure and the rules applying directly to individuals and associations and to be followed by them in particular transactions. If this division of labor can be established, individuals

and associations are then left free to advance their ends more effectively within the framework of the basic structure, secure in the knowledge that elsewhere in the social system the necessary corrections to preserve background justice are being made (Rawls 1996, pp. 268–269).[6]

In this division of labor, corporations fit under the broad category of associations of individuals, side by side with church congregations, book clubs, recreational sports leagues, and civil society organizations. However, an account of social systems that categorizes corporations alongside amateur softball teams and independent church congregations, and attributes to them similar responsibilities for the maintenance of a just society, would appear to inadequately differentiate between social categories.

Here, it is necessary to clarify the distinction between institutions and mere associations. Institutions may be understood as distinct systems of rules that govern the behavior of well-defined groups of people who share common ends, together with a mechanism for enforcing those rules with formal sanctions.[7] On this *intentional* account, institutions persist because of the intentions of the relevant agents whose interests they serve. An institution exists at a certain time and place where the rules it specifies are followed and enforced. The rules are enforced by members of the group who are empowered to act on behalf of the institution. All institutions are associations, but not all associations are institutions. Associations are perhaps best understood as collectives informed by collective purposes and shared norms.[8] Typically, associations have less rigid membership rules and informal, rather than formal, internal decision structures. Institutions may be either private or public depending on how one becomes a member and the nature of the sanctions. Private institutions include corporations, private universities, professional organizations, trade unions, and religious organizations. In private institutions, membership is determined by the members, and the primary sanction is the revocation of membership in the group. In many public institutions, membership is determined by nonmembers. Here, sanctions may include taxes, fines, the revocation of licenses, and imprisonment. Public institutions include regulatory agencies, public universities, and health care systems. Political institutions, such as legislative bodies and executive branch offices, are a subset of public institutions.

Private institutions operating within nations have distinctive resources and abilities that enable them to influence both the understanding of justice by citizens and the basic framework of society. In this way, private institutions are distinct from actual citizens or associations of citizens. The legitimate role of these institutions is unaccounted for in Rawls' characterization of the basic structure of society. Beyond the domestic sphere, Rawls' two-part division of labor also fails to adequately account for the roles of global institutions in our post-Wesphalian era. Global institutions are usefully separated into three categories. Multilateral organizations that are established by governments, such as the World Bank, International Monetary Fund, and the OECD; nongovernmental organizations such as the International Chamber of Commerce, Human Rights Watch, and Greenpeace; and transnational corporations and other business enterprises.

These three classes of global institutions share in common certain features that undermine Rawls' dualism. First, global institutions are operated or made functional by citizens of scores of nations who do not share allegiance to the same domestic government. They may be members of liberal societies, decent hierarchical societies, burdened societies, or benevolent absolutist societies; and many of these societies will have distinct, nonidentical conceptions of justice (Rawls 1999). Second, global institutions operate in a range of societies with different background conceptions of justice. The principles or values that should guide these institutions will not be informed by a either shared conception of justice on the part of the constituent members of these institutions or by a shared conception of justice in the societies in which the institutions function. What is needed are principles that can transcend these different conceptions of justice.

To more fully and fairly assess the adequacy of a Rawlsian account of global justice, we need to examine the subtle and carefully crafted arguments developed by Nien-hê Hsieh (2004, see also Hsieh 2009) in support of the claim that multinational enterprises based in developed economies have obligations of assistance to developing societies. Hsieh uses the arguments developed by Rawls in the *Law or Peoples* (1999) as the grounding for his arguments.

To facilitate our assessment of these arguments, it is necessary to introduce a basic distinction between the types of nations in which transnational business is conducted. Rawls provides a useful typology of societies, or "peoples," in his analysis of global justice. For our purposes, it will be sufficient to utilize a basic distinction he makes between two broad classes of "peoples." First, there are what Rawls characterizes as well-ordered societies. These are societies that operate according to liberal principles or meet certain conditions of decency. These conditions of decency include nonaggression, a shared conception of justice, and a system of law that respects human rights and that imposes other moral obligations on members of society derived from a shared conception of justice (Rawls 1999, pp. 64–67). Second, there are what Rawls calls burdened societies; that is, societies whose "historical, social, and economic circumstances make their achieving a well-ordered regime … difficult if not impossible" (Rawls 1999, p. 90). Hsieh argues that multinational corporations based in well-ordered societies, and largely owned by members of those societies, have an obligation to assist burdened societies in which they operate, so long as the assistance does not outweigh the benefits gained by these firms in the burdened society. However, this duty *only* applies when the well-ordered nation is *not* itself fulfilling its obligations regarding its duty of assistance to a specific burdened society.

This Rawlsian account of the duties of transnational companied has distinct limitations. These may be summarized with the observation that the account applies only to a limited number of transnational firms, only to limited segments of the global population, and only in certain timeframes. To better understand this assessment, consider the following: First, a large percentage of global populations live in well-ordered societies. For example, India constitutes a well-ordered society but has a large BoP population. On the political account, there is no duty of assistance to members of the BoP living in well-ordered societies; so there would appear to be no basis on the political account for an obligation on the part of corporations to BoP populations living in well-ordered societies such as India.[9] On this account, the obligations of justice are a feature of the needs of the societies in question and not a feature of the needs of individual members of a society.

Second, on the Rawlsian account, duties of assistance apply only to transnational companies that are largely owned by the members of the same well-ordered societies. However, in a globalized economy, ownership of transnational corporations is often multi-domestic with both individual and institutional investors from diverse societies owning shares of companies. Only a limited number of corporations will be largely owned by citizens of the nations in which they were founded or are based. Firms that fall outside of this group will not have any duties of assistance on this political account. Third, corporations may themselves be based in burdened societies; in which case, the duties of the firm toward the society in which it is based and toward other burdened societies are left unspecified.

Finally, the Rawlsian view fails to take into account the mobility of people and labor capital in the contemporary world. Many individuals do not live their lives within a single society but instead migrate across borders to escape poverty, conflict, or oppression. The International Labour Organization puts the number of migrant laborers alone at 100 million (International Labour Office 2010, p. 2). Again, what is needed is a theoretical structure that can provide principles that correspond to individual persons and not to societies or "peoples" (Buchanan 2000, p. 698). A Rawlsian account of global justice grounded in *Law of Peoples* does not provide such a framework. We need to look elsewhere.

Human Rights Cosmopolitanism

Moral cosmopolitanism may be said to have three distinct features, which it will be useful to summarize here:

> First, individualism: the ultimate units of concern are human beings, or persons – rather than, say, family lines, tribes, ethnic, cultural, or religious communities, nations, or states. The latter may be units of concern only indirectly, in virtue of their individual members or citizens. Second, universality: the status of ultimate unit of concern attaches to every living human being equally – not merely to some subset, such as men, aristocrats, Aryans, whites, or Muslims. Third, generality: this special status has global force. Persons are ultimate units of concern for everyone – not only for their compatriots, fellow religionists, or suchlike (Pogge 2002 a, b, p. 169).

There are a variety of moral cosmopolitan perspectives defended by moral and political philosophers, including consequentialist (Singer 1972, 2002; Unger 1996), Kantian (O'Neill 2000), needs-based (Brock 2009), and rights-based (Caney 2005; Pogge 2002 a, b, 2005). It is not possible or necessary to review and critically assess all of these alternatives to political accounts of global justice in this chapter. Instead, in this section, my aim is to defend a plausible cosmopolitan human rights perspective regarding the obligations of corporations and other business enterprises.

Much of the discussion that animates the flourishing literature on cosmopolitan justice concerns the specifications of the obligations that affluent individuals have to distant people living at the BoP. Strict cosmopolitans argue that duties of assistance are equally binding on members of one's community or nation as they are to distant others. Moderate cosmopolitans acknowledge that a duty of assistance to distant others is a binding obligation, but defend special obligations to local communities or nations that supersede obligations to distant others. The position defended in this section circumvents this debate altogether by focusing on the *relationships* that corporations and other business enterprises have to individuals. In particular, we will focus on the direct benefits and harms that may result from relationships with individuals as customers, as producers, as laborers, and as community members.[10] The argument developed here is thus limited in scope. In particular, the argument developed here does not address the obligations that businesses have, if any, to people with whom they do not have relationships.

The argument begins by drawing upon the literature on business and human rights. Within the business ethics literature, the obligation of corporations to respect human rights has been grounded in two complementary sets of arguments. First, corporate human rights duties are justified on contractualist grounds (Cragg 2002; Donaldson 1991). This argument, which Donaldson made persuasively over twenty years ago, takes into account the fact that the very reason that corporations are allowed to exist is to allow people to come together to make productive contributions to humanity. To accomplish this end, corporations are granted such rights as property and freedom in most nations. Corporate rights holders have reciprocal duties to respect the rights of others, including the basic human rights enjoyed by individual persons. Second, human rights are grounded in the idea that the human capacity of autonomous action entitles persons to basic respect, not merely from other individuals and governments, but from organizations with whom they have relationships. Together these two arguments provide an overlapping justification for the position that corporations operating transnationally have duties to respect human rights independently of the ability of host nation governments to police and remedy human rights transgressions by corporations. The idea that businesses have human rights obligations has also been institutionalized in recent years via a variety of international agreements and covenants among governments, multilateral organizations, and non-governmental organizations, culminating in the United Nations "'Protect, Respect and Remedy' Framework for Business and Human Rights" and its accompanying *Guiding Principles on Business and Human Rights* (2011) (see Chapter 4).

If such human rights duties can be justified, the question of the scope of these obligations must be addressed. Florian Wettstein defends an account of the human rights obligations of corporations where the obligations of corporations are limited only by their capabilities. On this account, corporations have expansive obligations to make "positive contributions to human development" consistent with their expertise and resources (Wettstein 2009; see also Wettstein 2012a, Wettstein 2012b). According to Wettstein, corporations are "quasi-governmental" institutions and are required to meet state-like human rights obligations. This is a much more expansive view of the scope of corporate human rights obligations than has been defended historically by business ethics scholars and is not the position defended here. Rather, it stands as one point on a spectrum of possible accounts of corporate human rights obligations and may be contrasted with a libertarian account of these obligations at the opposite end of a spectrum.

On one libertarian conception of the human rights obligations of corporations, no rights are binding on corporations that are not legally required or contractually agreed upon. This argument holds that no obligations or responsibilities can be binding on the basis of a relationship one has entered into unless one has expressly agreed to fulfill those obligations. In other words, corporations can have no special obligations independent of contractual agreements stipulating those obligations or formal commitments to human rights standards. Samuel Scheffler has called this the "voluntarist objection" (Scheffler 2001). This judgment can be seen as informing a libertarian perspective on international business ethics.

To test the strength of the voluntarist objection, let us use the standard philosophical technique of testing our intuitions against an example; in this case, a variation of Peter Singer's (1972) classic drowning child example.[11] Imagine that you are a business person who has secured a difficult-to-obtain pitch meeting with a senior executive at a large firm. He has agreed to meet you at a new factory he is inspecting that is being completed outside of town in a valley that is mainly farmland. Securing the contract would generate significant new revenue for your company. The executive is known to be fastidious about both business attire and punctuality. You leave for the meeting wearing appropriate attire. As you are driving down a dirt road to the factory, you notice a young child struggling to keep her head above water in an irrigation pond. You stop, wade into the pond, and save the child. The child, who appears to be about four years old, is crying for her mother in Spanish, which you do not speak. You see no one else in the area and you cannot get mobile phone reception. Your clothes are ruined and you are late for your appointment with the executive. What should you do now?

According to the voluntarist, you have no special obligation to the child since you have not expressly agreed to care for the child. You are free to leave the child by the side of the road, and proceed to your business meeting despite there being no adults in the area. The voluntarist can fairly point out that you have already incurred costs in the form of ruined clothes and tardiness for your meeting, which will make it more challenging for you to close the deal. Is leaving the child by the side of the road the correct choice?

The voluntarist objection conflicts with most people's intuitions because a child left alone under these circumstances is vulnerable to injury or death. But what reason can be given for the view that you have an obligation to see that the child is safely turned over to appropriate authorities before proceeding about your business?

One explanation is what we will call the *principle of protecting the vulnerable*. According to this principle, when a person or organization stands in a relevant relationship to a vulnerable party. The person or organization has a special obligation to protect the vulnerable party from harm when they have the capacity to do so. Vulnerability, however, is a relative concept insofar as parties that are simply less intelligent, less skilled, less strong, or less competitive are vulnerable to harm or loss from individuals who are more intelligent, more skilled, stronger, or more competitive. As George Brenkert (1998) has noted in a different context, we are particularly concerned with people who are vulnerable because their cognitive abilities, social circumstances, or economic standing make it impossible, or nearly impossible, for them to protect their own interests and welfare in comparison to normal adults. Vulnerability on this view does not constitute mere weakness relative to another party, in which case, we would all count as vulnerable agents, but vulnerability relative to a relevant baseline standard. One useful standard for assessing human vulnerability is one's capability to function well.

Poverty and development scholars have shown that the lives of the global poor are characterized by malnourishment, poor health, high illiteracy rates and trade-offs between food, health care, and education. Members of the BoP in particular are socially and cognitively vulnerable as a result of their poverty and the lack of institutional frameworks that can provide BoP populations with social welfare services. The cognitive vulnerability of those living at the BoP is a feature of illiteracy or limited education. Social vulnerability is a result of poverty itself. A short-term "live for the moment" mentality contributes to unhealthy tobacco and alcohol consumption, which exacerbates incapacities to function well, especially among the 2.6 billion people living in moderate and extreme poverty. Opportunities for a decent life are limited from early childhood and contribute to a range of vulnerabilities that leave people living at the BoP susceptible to misfortune and predation, typically without recourse to social or economic safety nets.

On the other hand, corporations can provide direct benefits to the BoP. Utilizing a capabilities framework, which both Nussbaum and Sen characterize as a form of human rights theorizing (Nussbaum 2007; Sen 2005). We can helpfully distinguish between two different categories of empowerment. First, ventures that provide opportunities for the poor to improve their capability to function well. These opportunities may take the form of employment with decent working conditions consistent with ILO conventions, purchasing produce grown by BoP farmers, or providing entrepreneurial opportunities. They are characterized by the opportunity they present for individuals in the BoP to utilize their labor to improve their capability to function well by earning income. Second, BoP consumers may be benefitted by ventures that offer direct opportunities for them to function well by purchasing products or services, the use of which directly improves their well-being. Examples might include renewable energy sources and inexpensive water purification systems.

On the cosmopolitan account defended here, harmful exploitation of people living at the BoP takes place when corporations or other business enterprises take advantage of their cognitive, social, and economic vulnerabilities in ways that violate or undermine such basic human rights as subsistence, physical security, and freedom of movement and association. These ideas are developed more extensively in Chapter 5.

Conclusion

If the arguments presented here are correct, a cosmopolitan account of justice is better suited than a political account to help us understand how corporations and other business enterprises can act as agents of justice in ways that enhance organizational moral legitimacy. The task of defending a theoretical framework regarding international business ethics is a complex endeavor. This chapter has attempted to contribute to that end in four ways. First, it has been argued that corporations are properly understood as agents of global justice. Second, it has been argued that there are two domains of normative legitimacy relevant to role of corporations and other business enterprises in promoting global justice: the legitimacy of global governance institutions and the legitimacy of corporations and other business enterprises. The arguments of this chapter have focused on corporate legitimacy. The most prominent political conception of CSR present in the management literature defends an account of corporate moral legitimacy grounded in deliberative democracy. It has been argued that this account is unpersuasive because of objections regarding process and voice, as well as the potential consequences of such a model.

Rawls' influential conception of justice is an important alternative for those who believe that a political conception of CSR is viable. The arguments of this chapter challenge the assumption that Rawls' theoretical framework can provide a satisfactory account of the obligations of corporations regarding global justice. In place of a political conceptions of CSR, an ethical conception of CSR grounded in an appropriately modest set of duties tied to relationships with stakeholders in the organization is defended. This position is cosmopolitan in scope and grounded in overlapping arguments for human rights. This view, it has been argued, provides the most plausible account of the duties of corporations operating in the post-Wesphalian era. In the next chapter, we will further unpack this cosmopolitan perspectives.

Notes

1. Key works from this period include De George (1993), Donaldson (1991), Donaldson and Dunfee (1999), and Santoro (2000).
2. Held's concerns are broader than poverty reduction and include "health, child labour, trade union activity, environmental protection, stake-holder consultation and corporate governance."
3. For criticism of instrumental accounts of practical reasoning, see O'Neill (2000), chapters 1 and 2.
4. This concept of legitimacy was developed by Weber to analyze governments and has been extended to organizations by Suchman and others. A normative account of legitimacy provides a justification for beliefs regarding the legitimacy of governments or organizations. A descriptive concept of legitimacy characterizes what people do believe about organizations and explains why they believe an organization is legitimate or illegitimate (Suchman 1995).
5. For a Rawlsian perspective on the implications of the "basic structure" of the global institutional framework, see Beitz (1979). This work builds on the early

work of Rawls, rather than the later work of Rawls, which is the primary focus of our discussion in this section.

6.   A similar position is endorsed by Nagel (1991).

7.   See Elster (1989), and Rawls (1955, 1971, esp. 54–60). For a summary of the intentional view of institutions, see Pettit (1992, esp. pp. 614–617).

8.   Social norms are shared by a group of people and are partly sustained by their approval or disapproval. Social norms are enforced via informal sanctions and lack formal mechanisms of enforcement. See Elster (1989, pp. 113–123).

9.   It is also not clear what the political account has to say about the distinctive obligations of corporations based in poor, well-ordered nations to those living in burdened societies.

10. For present purposes, I am putting aside indirect impacts via positive and negative externalities. For discussion of direct vs. indirect harm, see Chapter 7.

11. Singer asks us to imagine what duty we have to rescue a young child that is drowning when doing so would have only minor negative consequences for ourselves. He then uses the intuitive judgment that our duty is to rescue the child as a basis for extrapolating to duties regarding the distant impoverished.

Chapter Three

Human Rights Cosmopolitanism

There is a long and rich history of theorizing on the nature, content, and ethical implications of human rights that extends at least as far back in intellectual history as Locke. In the latter half of the twentieth century, ethical theorists sought to clarify our understanding of human rights and corresponding duties. For example, Henry Shue famously and persuasively argued in 1980 that the distinction between so-called negative rights to be free from interference and so-called positive rights to certain goods or services is untenable, essentially rendering moot the idea that there can be duties regarding negative rights but no equivalent duties regarding positive rights (Lomasky 1987; Shue 1996). Basic rights take the form of side-constraints on actions, that is they are moral boundaries on the actions of agents.

The moral account of rights defended here draws from the work of human rights scholars, but is novel insofar as it argues that transnational companies (TNCs) are properly understood as duty bearers in addition to individuals or states. This account of human rights has four essential features that are defended in this chapter. First, human rights are claim rights against parties with whom one stands in a relationship such as workers and their employers or community members and the TNCs that operate in those communities. Second, human rights are ultimately grounded in human agency or the capacity of persons to govern themselves. Third, the human rights that TNCs and other business enterprises have duties to protect and respect are basic rather than aspirational. Finally, corporations are properly understood at intentional agents with duties to protect human rights. These features distinguish the minimalist, cosmopolitan approach defended here from other accounts of the duties of TNCs regarding human rights.[1]

The Ethics of Global Business, First Edition. Denis G. Arnold.
© 2023 John Wiley & Sons Ltd. Published 2023 by John Wiley & Sons Ltd.

Claim Rights

There are a variety of ways of conceptualizing corporate human rights obligations, and different ways of thinking about human rights naturally entail different sets of human rights obligations. Much of the apparent disagreement regarding corporate human rights obligations reflect differences in the types of rights at issue and in the way scholars conceptualize the responsibilities of corporations to preserve or promote justice. Unpacking these distinctions will go some way toward providing clarity regarding corporate human rights obligations.

In the broader academic literature and international discourse on rights, many different types of rights are discussed including natural rights, moral rights, political rights, human rights, and legal rights. There is often an overlap between such rights, as for example between rights claimed to be natural or moral in nature, but that are also legally protected by states. Many of these rights are properly encompassed under the broader category of claim rights. Claim rights entitle individuals to assistance from other parties in the form of protection against injury or death, the provision of help in cases of need, the performance of responsibilities previously agreed upon or legally required, or to compensation from harm cause.[2] The parties who have a responsibility to satisfy the claim rights are said to have duties or obligations to the rights holder. Human rights are typically examples of claim rights, but human rights can be conceptualized in different ways. In some cases, different conceptualizations of human rights are compatible, in other cases they are not. An employee's right to be free from corporeal punishment, to compensation consistent with the satisfaction of basic needs, and to be paid according to the terms of his or her contract are examples of claim rights. But who is the duty bearer in these cases? Is it the state in which the corporation operates? Is it the corporation? Or is it some other entity such as global governance institutions? The answer to these questions depends upon both the way in which human rights are conceptualized and the way in which corporate human rights obligations are understood. Broadly construed, conceptual analysis of human rights may be divided into two primary categories: *moral* rights and *political* rights. Both of these types of analysis can be influential in determining which rights are given legal protection.

Political rights play a variety of functions in the lives of citizens and in business. Individuals may enjoy the right to vote and the right to political speech, but such privileges are legitimately constrained at work where one's duties are determined by the actual or implicit contract with one's employer. Claim rights, on the other hand, carry greater weight than political rights. This is because claim rights have moral authority. Rights claims are not mere requests or sincere hopes. They are the ultimate rational basis for making a demand upon others. As Amartya Sen puts it, a "human rights approach demands that the acknowledged rights of everyone, in the form of respecting freedoms and corresponding obligations, must be given ethical recognition" (Sen 2009, p. 362). The unique nature of these sorts of claims has been powerfully summarized by Joel Feinberg. Human rights claims, Feinberg explains:

> can be urged, pressed, or rightly demanded against other persons. In appropriate circumstances the right-holder can "urgently, peremptorily, or insistently" call for his rights, or assert them authoritatively, confidently, unabashedly. Rights are not mere gifts or favors, motivated by love or pity, for which gratitude is the sole fitting response. A right is something that can be demanded or insisted upon without embarrassment or shame. When that to which one has a right is not forthcoming, the appropriate action is indignation; when it is duly given there is no reason for gratitude, since it is simply one's own or one's due that one received. A world with claim-rights is one in which all persons, as actual or potential claimants, are dignified objects of respect, both in their own eyes and in the view of others. No amount of love and compassion, or obedience to higher authority, or noblesse oblige, can substitute for those values (Feinberg 1973, pp. 58–59; quoted in Shue 1996, pp. 14–15).

In nations with regulator and governance gaps people still may legitimately claim that TNCs have a duty to meet basic human rights standards.

Grounding Rights in Human Agency

Human rights constitute legitimate claims against others, but the precise nature and content of claim rights are disputed, as are the duties of corporations and other businesses with respect to human rights. These disputes mirror disputes regarding the rights of individuals in relation to other individuals and to states where the specific entitlements of individuals and the specific obligations of duty bearers are contested. Such disputes have lead some scholars to dismiss the idea that *any* rights can be identified and even to compare an approach to human rights that regards rights as ethical claims grounded in theory to fundamentalist religion (Ignatieff 2001; Rorty 1993). For example, Ignatieff claims that "Foundational beliefs of all kinds have been a long-standing menace to the human rights of ordinary individuals" (Ignatieff 2001, p. 86). He includes accounts of human rights that ground rights in ethical theory as an example of this sort of "idolatry."

However, as Brian Schaefer has argued, the arguments of critics of a foundational approach to human rights, such as Ignatieff and Rorty, are self-contradictory (Schaefer 2005). This is because they themselves defend human rights by appealing to moral facts about humans, such as human dignity, and so thereby appeal to foundations to support their own views.[3] Implicit or explicit moral claims of this nature can be read in nearly all scholarly discussions of rights, regardless of the disciplinary background of the author. This is because "all sufficiently deep reasons for human rights either appeal directly to the idea of human agency or rely on the ideas that presuppose human agency" (Ci 2005, pp. 243–265).

At a minimum, human agency involves the ability to reflect on one's first-order desires or preferences at a second-order level and to determine for oneself which desires or preferences to act upon.[4] Agents are capable of making and following their own judgments and are not merely subject to the causal laws of nature. There are at least two distinct lines of arguments that may be utilized to derive rights from agency. Thomas Nagel characterizes these as intrinsic and instrumental lines of argument (Nagel 1995, pp. 83–107). The intrinsic view, accepted by Nagel and Robert Nozick, is Kantian in derivation and may be summarized by the claim that agents possesses a unique dignity as self-governing beings that must be respected (Kant 1990: 52; Nozick 1974, p. 62). Rights, according to this view, are basic features of morality. They are nonaggregative goods that recognize persons as "inviolable and independent subjects, whose status as members of the moral community is not exhausted by the inclusion of their interests as part of the general good" (Nagel 1995, p. 86).

The instrumental view has been defended by Loren Lomasky (1987) and James Griffin (2008), among others. Both Lomasky and Griffin argue that the goal-orientated nature of persons, and in particular their capacity to identify practical interests and long term projects, allows us to recognize the sort of human life that is worthwhile. Because persons have a fundamental interest in having the freedom, or liberty, to pursue these interests, and in a minimal provision of health, physical welfare, and education necessary to pursue goals, it is argued that we should protect these interests as rights (Griffin 2008, pp. 159–175). For our purposes, we need not side with only the intrinsic or only the instrumental view of human rights, but can instead regard them as complementary arguments that provide a two-pronged moral grounding of human rights.[5] As a matter of rational consistency, a person who recognizes that they are a moral being must acknowledge that other persons are moral beings whose rights must be respected. To avoid an irrational contradiction, assuming that one recognizes one's own rights, one must recognize the rights of other individuals with the same relevant characteristics. This applies to managers of TNCs just as it applies to every other person.

Basic Rights

The account of rights defended here is limited in scope to basic rights. In delimiting the scope of perfect duties of TNCs to *basic* human rights, my account is different from that of other business and human rights scholars who argue for more expansive business duties regarding human rights (Cragg 2002, 2004;

Wettstein 2010). Basic rights are those rights necessary for the attainment of other rights and without which it is not possible to live a decent human life (Shue 1996, pp. 18–20). For example, a basic right to subsistence is necessary before one can take advantage of a nonbasic right to education. Basic rights may be contrasted with aspirational rights, such as unlimited access to high-quality education and healthcare, that may foster a flourishing and fully realized human existence but are difficult, or impossible, to guarantee universally. Henry Shue has famously and persuasively defended three basic rights: (i) liberty of physical movement and social participation (Shue 1996, pp. 65–88); (ii) physical security (Shue 1996, p. 20); and (iii) subsistence, meaning "unpolluted air, unpolluted water, adequate food, adequate clothing, adequate shelter, minimal preventive public health care" (Shue 1996, p. 23). These basic rights are "everyone's minimum reasonable demands on the rest of humanity. They are the rational basis for justified demands the denial of which no self-respecting person can reasonably be expected to accept" (Shue 1996, p. 19). Perfect duties to respect basic human rights constrain the pursuit of ends, whether they are self-interested goals or projects pursued on behalf of other parties such as shareholders (Kant 1990; Thompson 1993). When they stand in the appropriate relationship to an obligation-bearer, persons have rationally justified rights-claims against them.

Basic rights take the form of side-constraints that bound the moral space in which duty bearers may pursue ends without unjustified interference by other agents or institutions (Arnold 2003b, pp. 164–167; Herman 1993). The duty to respect basic rights acts as a trump against agents, organizations, or institutions that would violate basic rights. Theorists with a wide range of commitments readily agree that there are basic rights to liberty and physical security and that other persons have a duty not to constrain the freedom of others, or physically harm them, without strong justification (Griffin 2008; Lomasky 1987; Nozick 1974; Sen 1990). The rights to freedom and security are necessary for agentic self-governance. For example, a worker cannot bargain effectively if he is forced to work against his will, or if he is prohibiting from associating with other workers, or if he is physically assaulted to dissuade him from joining a union.

Agentic conceptions of human rights also support welfare rights such as a basic right to subsistence.[6] Whereas liberty rights to be free from being constrained or assaulted hold against all who would cause such harm to others, it has been argued that welfare rights, such as the right to subsistence appear to hold only when certain relationships exist. For example, a minor child has legitimate rights-claims against her parents regarding the provision of food, clothing, and shelter. The morally legitimate ends of parents do not include actions that substantially undermine the physical security or normal development of their child.

In this context, consider the plight of the world's poorest people discussed in the previous chapter. If the world's poorest people have a claim-right to subsistence, who are the corresponding duty bearers? One answer is that everyone with even a modest level of affluence is a duty bearer. It has been argued, for example, that the affluent of the world have an obligation to donate all or nearly all of the income they would otherwise spend on nonessential goods to alleviate global poverty (Banerjee 2010, pp. 265–274; Singer 1972, pp. 229–243). But what is the grounding of such a relationship between the world's affluent and the world's poor? Should not proximity, comparative wealth, personal history, or future prospects play a role in assessing such relationships? If the appropriate sort of relationship between a rights-holder and an obligation-bearer cannot be specified, then how can the extant of the obligation be assessed? O'Neill puts the matter this way.

> Whereas liberty rights and their corresponding universal obligations fall on all if on any, universal rights to goods and services can only be realized by establishing one of many differing possible sets of burdensome special relationships .... Claimants who do not know who bears the counterpart obligation to rights they claim may grasp thin air; by contrast, obligation-bearers who are not bound to specific claimants can nevertheless make the construction of institutions that allocate tasks and identify claimants the first step towards meeting their obligations (O'Neill 1996, pp. 134–135).

One obligation that the world's affluent populations may hold in common is the obligation to ensure that global institutions that have a direct impact on poverty and economic development, such as the World Bank, the United Nations, and the International Monetary fund, operate in a manner consistent with the bounds of justice and in a way that respects basic rights (Shue 1988, pp. 687–704). However, in cases where special relationships *already* exist in the global economy, rights-claims are binding on specific obligation-bearers. This is a crucial point for the argument of this chapter, for wherever TNCs do business they are *already* in special relationships with a variety of stakeholders, such as workers, customers, and local communities. In their global operations and in their global supply chains, TNCs have a duty to respect those with whom they have relationships. At a minimum, then, TNC managers have duties to both ensure that they do not physically harm or illegitimately undermine the liberty of any persons, and the additional obligation to ensure that subsistence rights are met.[7]

There is a second moral grounding of the human rights obligations of corporations: a social contract model (Cragg 2004, 2009; Donaldson 1991). This model is distinct from, but compatible with, agentically grounded corporate human rights obligations. A unique feature of this analysis is that it is entirely focused on corporations and not derivative of more general theories of human rights. Cragg's version of the social contract theory of corporate human rights obligations begins with the historically grounded claim that the legal status of corporations is expressly designed to promote public goods and that the legal status of corporations is fluid, rather than static, adapting as it has historically to societal changes. Cragg argues that when a need arises to "rearticulate and reallocate responsibilities for ensuring that public expectations of reciprocal benefits is realised," such a reallocation is warranted to ensure the public interest and provide ongoing normative legitimacy for the corporate entity (Cragg 2004, p. 124). He points to the new, multi-actor model of economic globalization with its attendant governance gaps to explain how "under conditions of globalisation, respect for and a commitment to advance respect for human rights is both constitutive of the public good to which corporations have an obligation to contribute and empirically necessary if public goods are to result from commercial corporate activity in global markets" (Cragg 2004, p. 124). On this account, the normative legitimacy of the modern corporate form is predicated on the willingness of corporations and their managers to respect human rights in their global operations. A social contract model can be read as supplementing or overlapping with agentically grounded human rights arguments. In other words, these accounts are not mutually exclusive but provide compatible forms of justification for corporate human rights obligations.

TNCs as Duty Bearers

Some readers may be skeptical that TNCs have the ontological status necessary to be duty bearers. One might claim, for example, that TNCs are mere legal fictions established for the purpose of enhancing the economic interests of investors and do not possess the agency necessary to be duty bearers.[8] This is not the case. Each type of company described by Bartlett and Ghoshal in chapter one directs the behavior and operations of subsidiaries in host nations. Multinational companies may grant more autonomy to subsidiary companies than global companies, but each type of company has the ability to direct subsidiary operations via an internal decision structure and a transnational ethical infrastructure. The internal decision structure includes hierarchical lines of organizational responsibility, rules of procedure, and corporate policies (French 1979). The ethical infrastructure of a company includes corporate ethics and compliance managers, employee training, company values statements, employee assessment and incentives linked to policies and values, and communications about ethics and compliance (Tenbrunsel et al. 2003; Trevino and Nelson 2010). The existence of internal decision structures and ethical infrastructures helps us to understand how companies can exhibit intentionality (Arnold 2006; French, 1996) and why it makes sense to hold both companies and their executive leadership teams accountable for organizational behavior including ethical transgressions.

Intentionality, in the sense relevant here, is understood at the ability to plan future actions in a coordinated manner (Bratman 1987, 1999). More specifically, plans have two distinct features: (i) they are typically partial or incomplete and need to be filled in over time; (ii) plans typically have a hierarchical structure in which some plans are embedded in other plans. This type of intentionality exists at the individual, group, and organizational level, but at the group and organizational level planning is accompanied by coordination. Understanding how organizations such as companies exhibit intentionality is important for understanding claims regarding organizational ethical legitimacy.

Before explaining how companies exhibit intentionality, it will be helpful to illustrate the planning conception of intentionality at the individual and group levels. At the individual level, imagine that a manager takes an overseas business trip. She must formulate a plan that will get her there and act upon it with the support of her assistant. Formulating the plan will involve reflection and deliberation on the length of her stay, appropriate travel dates, appropriate flights, and so on. However, some things will be left open, such as how she will travel to the airport and where she will eat while overseas. Acting on her plan will involve making airline reservations, traveling to the airport, obtaining a visa, and so on. As the time of travel draws closer, other aspects of the plan will be filled in based on current information and prior adjustments to the plan.

Similar planning takes place by groups. To see this, imagine the manager is one of several business associates, all of whom live in different cities, who agree to travel to China to tour the factories of a potential new supplier. A mutual intention to travel comes into existence once all parties come to this decision. The associates coordinate their subplans to facilitate the end of evaluating the potential supplier. Each person is aware of the subplans of other members of the group necessary for the execution of the plan. The required level of knowledge will vary between individuals and further plans, such as how many cities they visit, may still need to be negotiated. These negotiations regarding subplans may continue after the group has begun to carry out their plan. If the group satisfies the criteria of intentionality in these ways, it is proper to say that it has a collective intention to travel to China to evaluate a potential new supplier.

Now consider this conception of intentionality as it applies to companies and other organizations. Consider the example of a company implementing a new anti-corruption program in all of its global operations. Bribery anywhere in the world is illegal for all companies conducting business in the United States under the Foreign Corrupt Practices Act and in the United Kingdom under the Bribery Act (consistent with the OECD Convention on Combating Bribery of Foreign

Officials in International Bribery Transactions). Conventions and laws make bribery illegal because bribery is widely understood to undermine economic development, human rights, and democracy. Transparency International, the respected anti-corruption organization, succinctly summarizes the reasons that bribery has been made illegal via regulations and conventions.

> Corruption impedes investment, undermines economic growth, diverts human-itarian assistance and reduces market opportunities for legitimate business. When government is for sale, it destroys public trust in democratic institutions and denies citizens, businesses, taxpayers, and consumers the benefit of open markets and fair competition. Corruption disproportionately burdens the poor, diverting scarce resources that could otherwise help lift millions out of poverty. It raises the costs of education, nutrition, clean water, and health care, often denying citizens these essential public services (Transparency International 2015).

How might a large TNC intentionally implement an anti-corruption policy?

Such a process might look something like the following: First, executives form a committee to oversee this process. The committee might include the company's chief ethics officer and representatives from the general counsel's office, internal auditing, human resources, and other areas. Coordination is accomplished in the different departments and divisions of the company and its subsidiaries. For example, the corporate ethics office develops the principles and practices that will guide company behavior, the training of employees, and coordinates the production of an anti-bribery handbook that described various scenarios and appropriate responses in each of the nations or regions in which the company operates. Human resources crafts disciplinary procedures for employees who violate the policy. Corporate communications ensures that all employees are informed of the anti-bribery policy, together with sanctions for violations, and so on. The coordination requirement is satisfied insofar as each person is aware of the subplans of other members of the group necessary for the execution of the plan. Again, the required level of knowledge will vary between individuals. Presumably each employee of the company will need to be made aware of both the anti-bribery policy and the corresponding disciplinary policy. Further plans may still need to be negotiated, such as how best to convince employees to comply with the new policy. These negotiations regarding sub-plans may continue after the group has begun to carry out their plan. If the criteria of intentionality are met in these ways, it is proper to say that company has a collective intention to create and institute a new anti-bribery program.

It might be argued that multinational companies, where subsidiaries exhibit more autonomy, would find the process of implementing a global anti-corruption policy more challenging than global companies because parent companies in multinationals exhibit less control than global companies where parent companies retain greater control. However, global companies have the advantage over multinational companies of deep knowledge of local contexts that may better facilitate education and training of subsidiary employees relative to the local context of corruption. In other words, both types of companies have strengths and weaknesses with regard to implementing standards globally. TNCs that are both responsive to national contexts and capable of leveraging parent company expertise in training, evaluation, monitoring, and enforcement of employee compliance with anti-corruption policies may have an advantage in the successful implementation of anti-corruption policies. However, each of the company structures in Bartlet and Ghoshal's typology (discussed in Chapter 1) is compatible with the development and implementation of corporate ethics policies.

It is because the implementation of company policies and practices are intentional in the way that has been described here that it is proper to hold companies and their leaders accountable for corporate activity. For example, consider Walmart's aggressive use of bribery throughout Mexico. Walmart de Mexico, the Walmart subsidiary in Mexico, allegedly used large payoffs made to governmental officials to circumvent the law and obtain permits to build its stores in culturally and environmentally sensitive locations (Barstow 2012; Barstow and von Bertrab 2012).[9] It is alleged to have spent at least $24 million on illegal bribes in an effort to grow faster and bigger than its competition while using fraudulent accounting to cover up the bribes. Walmart did this in a systematic and entrepreneurial manner, seeking out officials it could bribe rather than succumbing to extortion. When these activities were reported to Walmart headquarters, an initial investigation by its internal investigations team was undertaken, only to be quashed by senior executives. The executive in charge of Walmart de Mexico, identified in media reports as the influential force behind the bribery scheme, was promoted to vice chairman of Wal-Mart. The company did not self-disclose the illegal activity to the US Department of Justice until news reporters investigated the allegations. In response, Walmart was widely criticized by Mexican social justice advocates, institutional investors, corporate governance authorities, and nongovernmental organizations. The failure of the parent company to monitor and enforce its own anti-bribery policies at Walmart de Mexico, or to discipline those involved, further undermined Walmart's moral legitimacy which has already been undermined by its labor practices in the United States and in its global supply chains.

The Business Principles for Countering Bribery provide comprehensive guidance for TNCs seeking to implement strong compliance with international anti-bribery regulations (Hess 2011).[10] Many firms utilize these principles to combat bribery in their global operations. Criticism of Walmart is appropriate because Walmart de Mexico appears to have intentionally engaged in bribery as a strategy to gain competitive advantage in Mexico; the US parent company failed to put in place controls to prevent bribery by its subsidiary and instead rewarded the executive that oversaw the bribery scheme; and because

Walmart failed to address the problem internally or report the illegal activity to US or Mexican authorities when it was first discovered. Corporate intentionality for illegal behavior, as illustrated in this example, is utilized by governmental authorities for assessing culpability and determining appropriate sanctions for illegal activity. For example, it is utilized by US attorneys and judges to determine culpability and penalties under the Federal Sentencing Guidelines for Organizations.

After the bribery scheme was made public, Walmart promptly implemented a new plan for its global ethics and compliance programs. This included increasing its compliance staff by 30% and requiring that potential foreign corruption be reported to global corporate headquarters and the board of directors (Harris 2014).[11] This is an example of the reflective assessment of existing practices and the implementation of new plans that is a necessary condition of agency. It illustrates a typical example of organizational change, one that is grounded in a recognition that some external control agents are unwilling to tolerate misconduct and a recognition that maintaining organizational legitimacy requires that the firm alter its current practices and implement new plans.

Meeting human rights obligations can be understood as a central element of the ethics and compliance programs of TNCs, just as implementing anticorruption programs are for many companies. It might be thought that because TNCs have human rights obligations, they should also be understood as rights bearers.[12] Agency is not, however, a sufficient condition for personhood. As explained in the following section, persons in the ontological (not legal) sense have freedom of the will, the capacity to gain meaning, personal satisfaction, and happiness, from the pursuit of plans and life projects, and the moral status of ends in themselves. These characteristics are not shared by corporations, but these characteristics are essential features of moral justifications of human rights.[13] This unique status of human persons is recognized in the *Universal Declaration of Human Rights*, which is explicitly grounded in the "dignity and worth of the human person" and which makes repeated use of the concept of human dignity. Mere agents, in contrast, possess none of these qualities. For example, a sophisticated computer that exhibited agency, but did not have freedom of the will, nor the capacity to gain meaning, personal satisfaction, and happiness, from the pursuit of plans and life projects, would not qualify as a person entitled to human rights, even if it was granted the status of legal personhood.

Finally, even if one rejects the view that corporations are properly regarded as intentional agents and duty bearers, one can readily acknowledge that all corporations are populated by individual employees who are agents and, as such, are duty bearers. If individual moral agents have a duty to respect basic human rights, then absent an argument to the contrary, those duties carry over to their work for companies. We do not normally hold that doctors, or military personnel, or members of religious orders, are exempt from human rights duties by virtue of their occupations, so it is not clear what an argument would look like that exempted business persons from basic human rights duties because of their roles as managers or executives.

To sum up, TNCs are properly understood as corporate moral agents capable of being duty bearers and entities morally responsible for their actions because they have internal decision structures comprised of human agents, including the ethical infrastructure of the firm, corporate intentions understood primarily as plans, and the capacity for reflective assessment of corporate plans and practices.

Human Rights as Political Rights

As we have seen, both an agentically ground theory and a social contract theory can provide a moral grounding for corporate human rights obligations. Political accounts of human rights, on the other hand, eschew moral justifications and instead appeal to the role rights play in the international political sphere.[14] Political accounts of human rights focus on theoretical or actual agreements among nations (or 'peoples' in Rawls idiosyncratic theory) and supranational organizations such as the United Nations and the International Labour Organization. The historical function of international human rights law has been to provide universal standards for the treatment of individuals by national governments. In practice, the current international human rights legal system includes, at a minimum, the Universal Declaration of Human Rights, the International Covenant on Economic, Social and Cultural Rights, the International Covenant on Civil and Political Rights, and the International Labour Conventions.[15] While moral rights may be used to justify some or all of international human rights law, international human rights can be justified independently of a direct correlation to morally justified human rights.[16]

While the system of international human rights emerged in the twentieth century with the explicit goal of protecting individuals against abuses by states, the system of human rights has evolved to take into account the obligations of supranational organizations such as corporations and multilateral organizations. As Andrew Clapham explained decades ago, "the supranational factor has meant that the individual-State dichotomy is no longer sufficient to explain complex relations in modern society … supranational organs introduce a new power relationship with potential for abuse of power between the individual and the supranational authority" (Clapham 1993). TNCs operate in a multitude of political jurisdictions and so are subject to a multitude of legal frameworks. Laws regarding such matters as the treatment of customers, the treatment of employees, and environmental protection vary significantly in different host nations. In the case of developing economies, consumer protection, worker safety, and environmental safeguards are often poorly developed and enforced. The law enforcement infrastructure and judicial apparatus necessary to ensure compliance is often weak, understaffed, and underfunded. TNCs operating in such nations are often free to determine for themselves whether or not they will adhere to host nation laws.

Observers of a post-Westphalian international system note an increase in the influence and power of corporations and an inability on the part of governments to appropriately govern corporate operations and impacts.[17] For example, Stephen Kobrin argues that "the shift from a state-centric to multi-actor system associated with the emergence of a transnational world order has fragmented political authority and blurred the once distinct line between the public and private spheres: both have led to an expanded conception of the rights and duties of non-state actors" (Kobrin 2009, p. 353). It is because of actual corporate human rights abuses, and not merely the potential for such abuses, that the United Nations developed and approved the "'Protect, Respect and Remedy' Framework for Business and Human Rights" and its accompanying *Guiding Principles on Business and Human Rights*.[18] We turn our attention to the new, internationally sanctioned business and human rights framework in the next chapter.

Conclusion

We have seen that TNCs have the kind of ontological status necessary for moral agency and moral responsibility and that they are capable of ignoring human rights obligations or of integrating human rights protections into their international operations. It has been argued that there are compelling reasons to believe that TNCs have agentically grounded moral obligations to respect basic human rights and that there are also sound social-contract-based arguments for concluding that businesses have human rights obligations. The international legal system of human rights includes explicit expectations for TNCs to respect the international human rights regime. As we shall see in the next chapter, this is an obligation endorsed by mainstream business organizations, as well as individual companies and by most national governments.

Notes

1. See, for example, Donaldson, T. (1991). *The Ethics of International Business*. Oxford: Oxford University Press. Santoro, M.A. (2000). *Profits and Principles: Global Capitalism and Human Rights in China*. Cornell University Press; Wettstein, F. (2009). *Multinational Corporations and Global Justice: Human Rights Obligations of a Quasi Governmental Institution*. Stanford, CA: Stanford University Press.
2. For the classic analysis of right as claims see Feinberg, J. (1966). Duties, rights, and claims. *American Philosophical Quarterly* 3 (2): 137–144; see also Arnold, D.G., Audi, R. and Zwolinski, M. (2010). Recent work in ethical theory and its implications

for business ethics. *Business Ethics Quarterly* 20 (4): 559–558; Beitz, C.R. (2009). *The Idea of Human Rights*. New York: Oxford University Press; Wenar, L. (2005). The nature of rights. *Philosophy & Public Affairs* 33 (3) 223–252. Wenar defends a framework for understanding the nature of all rights that is divided into four basic types and two categories. The two categories are first-order rights over one's mind and body and second-order rights over first-order rights. The four types of rights are privileges, claims, powers, and immunities.

3.   Brian, S. (2005). Human rights: problems with the foundationless approach. *Social Theory and Practice* 31 (1): 1–24, 6. Schaefer also argues that a foundationless approaches to human rights cannot be implemented universally without violating the very values associated with rights by means of coercion against individuals and cultures that are "rights-resistant." In order to implement human rights regimes in rights-resistant cultures, such cultures, or nations, will need to be coerced into compliance with economic or military means, thereby undermining the autonomous decision making of leaders of the culture or nation that is rights-resistant. In contrast, Schaefer argues, appeals to moral facts about humans provide rational grounds for persuading those who are rights-resistant that rights should be respected (15).

4.   For a defense of this account of personhood, see (Dworkin 1988; Frankfurt 1988). For more recent discussion of the hierarchical conception of personhood, see (Kane 1998). For an important discussion of the relationship of personhood to rights, see (Melden 1977). The question of what rights humans with severe mental impairment may be said to have is a complex issue. Addressing this important topic is, however, beyond the scope of this essay.

5.   Simon Caney employs a similar approach in his important recent discussion of the human rights implications of global climate change. See (Caney 2009, pp. 69–90).

6.   Both (Griffin 2008; Lomasky 1987) defend this position. There remains some controversy, mainly on the part of libertarians, over whether or not there are so-called positive rights to certain economic and social goods but Lomasky (himself a libertarian), following Shue, persuasively argues against such as distinction.

7.   For a different perspective on the grounding of TNC human rights duties, see (Santoro 2000, 2010, pp. 285–297).

8.   It worth noting that if this position were accepted as accurate most normative work in business ethics would be undermined since all normative business ethicists operate with the view that businesses are capable of ethical or unethical conduct at some level.

9.   This account of Walmart's alleged actions in this section is based on the Pulitzer Prize winning investigative reporting of David Barstow and Alejandra Xanic von Bertrab. The US Department of Justice has not yet determined; Walmart's culpability. However, regardless of its accuracy the account presented by Barstow and von Bertrab can be used to illustrate the account of corporate agency that is our concern in this section. See Barstow, D. (2012). Vast Mexico Bribery case hushed up by Wal-Mart after top-level struggle. *The New York Times* (22 April 2012), A1; Barstow, D. and Xanic Von Bertrab, A. (2012). "The Bribery aisle: how Wal-Mart got its way in Mexico. *The New York Times* (18 December 2012), A1.

10. David Hess, "Partnering against corruption initiative and the business principles for countering Bribery" in Thomas Hale and David Held (eds.), *The Handbook of Transnational Governance: Institutions and Innovations* (Cambridge: Polity Press, 2011) 322–327.

11. Harris, E.A. (2014). After bribery scandal, high-level departures at Walmart". *The New York Times* (5 June 2014), B1.

12. John D. Bishop, "The limits of corporate human rights obligations and the rights of for-profit corporations" (2012) 22:1 *Business Ethics Quarterly* 119–144.

13. These characteristics of human persons are explained in detail below. Amy Sepinwall (note 2, pp. 523–524) uses human rights theory to argue against the idea that corporate moral agency is philosophically distinct from corporate moral personhood and thereby susceptible to the criticisms levelled against corporate moral personhood. However, in doing so she ignores each of these features of moral accounts of human rights. It is only because she ignores these essential features of moral accounts of human rights that her use of human rights theory to deny the possibility of a distinction between agency and personhood may seem plausible. But the account of human rights theory she presents is partial and incomplete. Once this mistake is recognized and a full account is provided, her argument for denying the distinction fails. Nonetheless, she provides pragmatic moral and political reasons for thinking that corporations should be regarded as morally and legally responsible agents that are compatible with the ontological argument provided here.

14. Beitz, note 18; Buchanan, A.E. (2013). *The Heart of Human Rights*. New York: Oxford University Press; Rawls, J. (1999). *Law of Peoples*. Cambridge, MA: Harvard University Press.

15. While the ILO Conventions are not a part of the International Bill of Human Rights, they are an important element of the international human rights legal system and are particularly important to discussions of corporate human rights obligations because employers' representatives (along with workers' representatives and government representatives) are a formal component of the ILO governance structure. The United Nations "Protect, Respect and Remedy" Framework expressly refers to both the International Bill of Rights and the ILO Conventions.

16. Buchanan provides a compelling argument for the conclusion that the international legal system of human rights can be provided with a robust, pluralistic moral justification (that includes, among many other elements, the normative justification of the institutions and practices that create the system). Buchanan, A.E. (2009). *Human Rights, Legitimacy, and the Use of Force*. New York: Oxford University Press; Buchanan (2013), note 29, 14–22.

17. For helpful reviews, see Cragg (2009; Santoro, M.A. (2010). Post-Westphalia and its discontents: business, globalization, and human rights in political and moral perspective. *Business Ethics Quarterly* 20 (2): 285–297.

18. The United Nations "Protect, Respect and Remedy" Framework, summarized by the *Guiding Principles*, was developed by the Special Representative of the Secretary-General on the issue of human rights and transnational corporations and other business enterprises and endorsed by the Human Rights Council in its resolution 17/4 of June 16, 2011.

Chapter Four

The United Nations Business and Human Rights Framework

The legal system of international human rights emerged in the twentieth century with the explicit goal of protecting individuals against abuses by states. In practice, the current international human rights legal system includes, at a minimum, the Universal Declaration of Human Rights, the International Covenant on Economic, Social and Cultural Rights, the International Covenant on Civil and Political Rights, and the International Labour Conventions. However, as we have seen, the supranational status of transnational companies, and the potential abuse of power by transnational companies (TNCs) in relation to individuals, requires that TNCs be addressed in the contemporary international system of human rights (Clapham 1993, p. 138). TNCs operating in the global economy support human rights by providing jobs with compensation adequate for a decent standard of living, safe and healthy working conditions, products and services beneficial to humanity, and by demonstrating respect for the rule of law. TNCs operating in the global economy also violate human rights by providing below subsistence compensation, unsafe working conditions, harmful environmental pollution, engaging in bribery, harming indigenous populations, and by ignoring host nation laws. An examination of 65 sample cases of egregious human rights violations that were alleged by nongovernmental organizations (NGOs) to have been committed by TNCs found that oil, gas, and mining companies were involved most often, followed by the food and beverage sector, the apparel and footwear sector, and the information technology sector.[1] In response to several lawsuits alleging TNC human rights violations, US courts have found that TNCs may be held liable for complicity in human rights violations abroad (Muchlinsk 2001, pp. 31–47). Thousands of TNCs and other business enterprises have publicly committed to protecting human rights by signing the United Nations (UN) Global Compact. Many TNCs,

The Ethics of Global Business, First Edition. Denis Arnold.
© 2023 John Wiley & Sons Ltd. Published 2023 by John Wiley & Sons Ltd.

lead by the Business Leaders Initiative on Human Rights (BLIHR), now incorporate human rights polices into their codes of conduct and operations.

In a 2005 mandate, the UN Commission on Human Rights created the position of Special Representative of the Secretary General on the issue of Human Rights and Transnational Corporations and Other Business Enterprises (SRSG) in order to clarify various aspects of the Global Compact.[2] In a series of reports and supporting documents, the SRSG has articulated a tripartite framework regarding business and human rights that has three core principles: "the State duty to protect against human rights abuses by third parties, including business; the corporate responsibility to respect human rights; and the need for more effective access to remedies."[3] Operating in the spirit of pragmatic engagement, and in a manner consistent with the aims of the 2005 mandate of the UN Commission on Human Rights that created the position, this chapter clarifies the corporate responsibility, or duty, to respect human rights and to provide a moral foundation for that duty. The mission and aims of the SRSG's team is directly linked to the work previously undertaken by the UN on business and human rights. The first section of this chapter examines the recent history of the UN in regard to business and human rights and places the tripartite framework in that context. It argues that the previous effort to articulate the human rights duties of TNCs by the UN Working Group on the Methods and Activities of TNCs, which is the work of the SRSG supplants, is rightly rejected for three distinct reasons. Section two of the chapter analyzes the tripartite framework and argues that the grounding of the duty of TNCs to respect human rights is moral, not merely political or strategic. Section three of the chapter provides an account of basic human rights, in contrast to aspirational rights, and defends a moral account of the duty of TNCs to respect basic human rights. The main conclusion of the chapter is that only a moral account of the basic human rights duties of TNCs provides a sufficiently deep justification of "the corporate responsibility to respect human rights" feature of the SRSG's framework to provide reasons for universal acceptance, compliance, and enforcement of those duties.

Recent United Nations Initiatives on Business and Human Rights

The Global Compact

In 2000, the United Nations Secretary General Koofi Annan introduced the Global Compact as a policy initiative and practical framework for responsible business activity in the world economy (United Nations Global Compact Office 2008). The UN Global Compact "asks companies to embrace, support and enact, within their sphere of influence, a set of core values in the areas of human rights, labour standards, the environment, and anti-corruption" (Figure 4.1) (United Nations Global Compact Office 2008). Principles 1 and 2 of the Global Compact are explicitly concerned with the human rights duties of businesses. Principle 1 holds that "Businesses should support and respect the protection of internationally proclaimed human rights" and Principle 2 holds that "businesses must make sure that they are not complicit in human rights abuses." Approximately 10 000 companies in 166 nations have pledged to adhere to the 10 principles of the Global Compact.[4]

The Global Compact has both conceptual and practical limitations that inhibit its usefulness as a tool for civil regulation. Self-regulation occurs when a company or industry promulgates and pledges to adhere to principles or a code of ethical behavior (Levis 2006, pp. 50–55). Civil regulation occurs when a nongovernmental organization promulgates a set of principles, or code of conduct, for businesses and partners with businesses in an effort to secure

---

Human rights
- Principle 1: Businesses should support and respect the protection of internationally proclaimed human rights; and
- Principle 2: make sure that they are not complicit in human rights abuses.

Labour standards
- Principle 3: Businesses should uphold the freedom of association and the effective recognition of the right to collective bargaining;
- Principle 4: the elimination of all forms of forced and compulsory labour;
- Principle 5: the effective abolition of child labour; and
- Principle 6: the elimination of discrimination in respect of employment and occupation.

Environment
- Principle 7: Businesses should support a precautionary approach to environmental challenges;
- Principle 8: undertake initiatives to promote greater environmental responsibility; and
- Principle 9: encourage the development and diffusion of environmentally friendly technologies.

Anti-corruption
- Principle 10: Businesses should work against corruption in all its forms, including extortion and bribery.

Figure 4.1   The 10 principles of the United Nations Global Compact.
Source: United Nations Global Compact Office (2008).

compliance with the principles or code (Muchlinski 2007, p. 550). Among the factors that limit the effectiveness of the Global Compact are the following. (i) A lack of definitional clarity on key concepts such as "sphere of influence" and "complicity" in human rights abuses; (ii) a lack of clarity on the distinct duties of corporations and other business enterprises as opposed to nation states; (iii) limited guidance regarding how to measure and report on compliance with the principles; and (iv) a lack of penalties or repercussions for failing to adhere to the principles beyond being delisted for failing to file annual progress reports (Deva 2008, pp. 107–151). As we shall see, most of these difficulties have been readily acknowledged by the UN itself.

Norms on the Responsibilities of Transnational Corporations

Coincidental with the introduction of the Global Compact, the UN Sub-Commission on the Promotion and Protection of Human Rights was investigating the role of businesses enterprises in the promotion and protection of human rights. In 1998, the Sub-Commission appointed a sessional Working Group on the Methods and Activities of Transnational Corporations to conduct relevant background research and to draft a code of conduct for transnational corporations. In 2003, the Working Group presented the Sub-Commission with "Norms on the Responsibilities of Transnational Corporations and Other Business Enterprises with Regard to Human Rights" (Appendix) (Weissbrodt and Kruger 2003, pp. 901–922). The Norms were endorsed by scores of nongovernmental organizations including Amnesty International, Human Rights Watch, and the Prince of Wales International Business Leaders Forum (Weissbrodt and Kruger 2003, p. 906). However, business organizations, including the International Chamber of Commerce (ICC), the International Organisation of Employers (IOE), and the U.S. Council for International Business harshly criticized the Norms and expressed skepticism that the Norms would constructively facilitate the shared goal of human rights protection (International Chamber of Commerce and the International Organisation of Employers 2003; United States Council for International Business undated).

The Norms have three distinctive characteristics that distinguish them from previous international codes of corporate conduct such as the International Labour Organisation (ILO) Tripartite Declaration of Principles Concerning Multinational Enterprises (1977, 2000), the World Health Organization (WHO) Ethical Criteria for Medicinal Drug Promotion (1986), the UN's earlier draft Code of Conduct on Transnational Corporations (1984), and the Organisation for Economic Cooperation and Development (OECD) Guidelines for Multinational Enterprises (2000). First, the Norms unified and integrated principles articulated in international codes of conduct for transnational corporations and other businesses adopted by the OECD, ILO, and WHO, as well as general human rights agreements such as the UN Universal Declaration of Human Rights (1948), the UN Rio Declaration on the Environment and Development (1992), the WHO Health for All Policy for the Twenty-First Century (1998), and the UN World Summit on Sustainable Development Plan of Development (2002). In this way "the Norms largely reflect, restate, and refer to existing international norms" (International Chamber of Commerce and the International Organisation of Employers 2003).

There are several difficulties to such an approach to addressing the human rights duties of TNCs. First, in compiling codes or principles intended for both states and TNCs, the Norms failed to differentiate between two fundamentally different agents of global justice: nations and corporations. Nation states control specific geographic domains; tax and regulate industry; grant patents, copyrights, mineral and water rights; provide security via military forces; and negotiate treaties with the main purpose of serving national interests. TNCs purchase and own property; pay taxes; are regulated; receive patents, copyrights, mineral and water rights; supply military hardware; and are subject to the constraints of treaty negotiations with the main purpose of increasing private wealth. One can acknowledge that the distinction is sometimes blurred, as in the cases of the East India Company or the United Fruit Company on the one hand and state-owned enterprises on the other hand, without undermining the core distinction. Failing to distinguish between these two different types of agents, with their distinct purposes and practices, results in confusion regarding human rights duties, undermines the integrity of the Norms, and thereby undermines efforts to enhance respect for human rights by multiple agents of justice in the global arena.

Second, the Norms are aspirational in the sense that they identify ideals of TNC behavior rather than minimum standards of acceptable international conduct. In this sense, the Norms parallel the Universal Declaration of Human Rights in articulating ideal human rights standards. For example, among the articles are the following:

12. Transnational corporations and other business enterprises shall respect civil, cultural, economic, political, and social rights, and contribute to their realization, in particular the rights to development; adequate food and drinking water; the highest attainable standard of physical and mental health; adequate housing; privacy; education; freedom of thought, conscience, and religion; and freedom of opinion and expression; and refrain from actions which obstruct or impede the realization of those rights.

14. Transnational corporations and other business enterprises shall carry out their activities in accordance with national laws, regulations, administrative practices, and policies relating to the preservation of the environment of the countries in which they operate as well as in accordance with relevant international agreements, principles, objectives, responsibilities, and standards with

regard to the environment as well as human rights, public health and safety, bioethics, and the precautionary principle; and shall generally conduct their activities in a manner contributing to the wider goal of sustainable development.

The requirement in Article 12 that TNCs contribute to "the highest attainable standard" of physical and mental health, adequate housing, and education implies that TNCs must promote a range of social goods that wealthy nations such as the United States have difficulty providing for their citizens. Aside from being a moving target, since what is attainable will depend on available resources and technologies and will evolve over time, the Norms fail to provide specific guidance about what constitutes such complex ends as "mental health" and "education." The requirement in Article 14 that TNCs "shall carry out their activities in accordance with "bioethics" and the "precautionary principle" is equally imprecise insofar as the vast range of claims or duties that might fall under the umbrella of bioethics is left unspecified in the article and in the Sub-commissions official commentary on the Norms. The difficulty of properly understanding the precautionary principle is well understood, but not well articulated or defended by the Sub-Commission (Sunstein 2003, pp. 449–460). As the ICC and the IOE note, "the Norms "extend far beyond issues of basic human rights and cover a wide range of political, social, and economic rights that should be decided by national governments. It would be highly inappropriate to privatize, in effect, the policing of those rights by making companies the enforcing agent" (International Chamber of Commerce and the International Organisation of Employers 2003).

Third, the drafters of the Norms claim that the Norms are nonvoluntary and thus that they are legally binding. The nonvoluntary nature of the Norms is said to be reflected in the implementation provisions that require reporting and oversight (Weissbrodt and Kruger 2003, p. 913). According to David Weisbrodt, principle drafter of the Norms:

> The legal authority for the Norms derives principally from their sources in treaties and customary international law, as a restatement of international legal principles applicable to companies. The United Nations has promulgated dozens of declarations, codes, rules, guidelines, principles, resolutions, and other instruments, in addition to treaties, that interpret the general human rights obligations of member states under Article 55 and 56 of the Charter and may reflect customary international law. The Universal Declaration of Human Rights is the most prominent of those instruments; it not only serves as an authoritative, comprehensive, and nearly contemporaneous interpretation of the human rights obligations under the Charter, but also contains provisions that have been recognized as reflective of customary international law (Weissbrodt and Kruger 2003, p. 913).

In the view of the Sub-Commission, the Norms constituted "soft law," which they take to mean nonvoluntary guidelines, but can be expected to evolve into "hard law" via treaties and other means (Weissbrodt and Kruger 2003, pp. 914–915). The ICC, IOE, and USCIB rejected the claim that the Norms were nonvoluntary. "By calling them "nonvoluntary" and using legal language where there is no legal obligation, the draft "norms" blur the line between voluntary and legal actions, and make corporate compliance virtually impossible."[5] By asserting that a complex, vague, and non-bounded set of norms is legally binding, while recognizing that existing international law does not support such an interpretation, the Sub-Commission overreached and undermined its credibility in the business community and elsewhere.

The Norms are an example of what Onora O'Neill describes as "the dark side of human rights" (O'Neill 2005, pp. 427–439). By this she means both the "cornucopia of universal human rights" that has been promulgated by national and international bodies and the associated expectation that states must secure respect for these rights through various regulatory means (O'Neill 2005, pp. 428, 433). But as O'Neill argues, the complexity of the task involved in promulgating and enforcing long, complicated, lists of rights – such as those articulated in the Norms – is counterproductive to the achievement of the core goal of a decent or respectful standard of life for all (O'Neill 2005, p. 439).

> Those of whom too much that is extraneous to their basic tasks … is required are likely to resent the proliferating and time-consuming requirements to obtain permissions, to consult third parties, to record, to disclose, to report, and to comply with the demands of inspectors or regulators. These requirements for control and accountability impose heavy human and financial costs, and are often damaging to the performance of primary tasks (O'Neill 2005, p. 437).

The critique of the Norms offered here is not that the task of articulating and defending core corporate human rights duties is hopeless, rather the critique is that the Norms failed to provide a plausible and defensible account of those duties and in so doing undermined, rather than enhanced, efforts to ensure that corporations contribute to the fulfillment of those basic human rights necessary for a decent work experience and standard of living for all.[6]

The Work of UN Special Representative to the Secretary General

Lacking strong support from business groups or states, the UN Commission on Human Rights failed to endorse the Norms. However, a need remained for clarification of the Global Compact and its human rights standards. In 2005, the Commission requested that the UN Secretary General appoint a Special Representative to the Secretary General on the Issue of Human Rights and Transnational Corporations and Other Business Enterprises with a mandate regarding business and human rights that included the identification of standards of responsibility and accountability of TNCs with regard to human rights.[7] John Ruggie was appointed as the SRSG and he and his team undertook background research and multi-stakeholder consultations. With respect to the inevitable normative judgments that must be made in fulfillment of the mandate, the SRSG largely eschewed theory and embraced what he describes as "principled pragmatism" characterized as "an unflinching commitment to the principle of strengthening the promotion and protection of human rights as it relates to business, coupled with a pragmatic attachment to what works best in creating change where it matters most - in the daily lives of people."[8] The SRSG team articulated a tripartite account of the duties of TNCs and states with respect to human rights. The framework holds that states have the primary duty to *protect* against human rights abuses by third parties including TNCs, that TNCs and other business enterprises have a duty to *respect* human rights, and that access to *remedy* must be made available to victims of human rights abuses.[9] The objective of the SRSG team was to produce a framework for understanding the duties of TNCs and other business enterprises regarding human rights that avoids the errors of the Norms and succeeds in appealing to a broader range of constituencies than did the Norms. The result is the "'Protect, Respect and Remedy' Framework for Business and Human Rights" and its accompanying *Guiding Principles on Business and Human Rights*.[10]

The framework recommended by the SRSG was approved by the UN Human Rights Council (successor of the UN Human Rights Commission) in 2006 and subsequently incorporated in the OECD *Guidelines for Multinational Enterprises*. Significantly for understanding the normative legitimacy of the *Guiding Principles*, business organizations were active in development of the "Protect, Respect, and Remedy" framework. The tripartite framework and the *Guiding Principles* were expressly endorsed by the International Organisation of Employers, the International Chamber of Commerce, and the Business and Industry Advisory Committee to the OECD. These organizations, and other business organizations and specific companies, also played a consulting role during the six-year development process of the tripartite framework. However, the framework provides only voluntary guidance and the UN Human Rights Council has been criticized by nongovernmental organizations such as Human Rights Watch for failing to implement a mechanism for assessing the compliance of firms with the framework (Human Rights Watch 2011).

The Tripartite Framework

The SRSG grounds the tripartite framework on the foundation of the state duty to protect against human rights abuses by third parties including TNCs and other business enterprises. "The human rights regime rests upon the bedrock role of States. That is why the duty to protect is a core principle of the business and human rights framework."[11] In order to strengthen human rights protections against corporate violations, the SRSG recommends a variety of enhanced domestic policies to encourage respect for human rights by TNCs and to hold them accountable for both domestic and non-domestic human rights violations. Among these policy recommendations are support for corporate cultures that respect human rights through sentencing practices that tie an evaluation of corporate cultures to criminal liability and punishment; tighter control of state owned enterprises; trade policy and human rights policy alignment; implementation of regulations that are applicable to TNCs when operating outside their home nations; and greater international cooperation in order to harmonize standards.[12]

The second part of the framework is the TNCs "baseline responsibility ... to respect human rights."[13] This responsibility is said to be grounded both in "social expectations" and in prudential risk management.[14] According to the SRSG, "Failure to meet this responsibility can subject companies to the courts of public opinion - comprising employees, communities, consumers, civil society, as well as investors – and occasionally to charges in actual courts."[15] The SRSG holds that both passive and active measures, such as corporate training programs, are required to protect human rights in order to do no harm.[16] In order to discharge this responsibility, due diligence processes such as those carried out in support of financial transactions and legal compliance are required. Three factors are to be considered in carrying out due diligence:

> The first is the country contexts in which their business activities take place, to highlight any specific human rights challenges they may pose. The second is what human rights impacts their own activities may have within that context - for example, in their capacity as producers, service providers, employers, and neighbours. The third is whether they might contribute to abuse through the relationships connected to their activities, such as with business partners, suppliers, State agencies, and other non-State actors. How far or how deep this process must go will depend on circumstances.[17]

The third and final feature of the human rights framework is access to remedy. The SRSG recognizes the importance of access to remediation in cases where human rights are violated. States must provide "mechanisms to investigate, punish, and redress abuses" through both judicial and non-judicial means such as health and safety agencies and public mediation services.[18] The SRSG also recommends that TNCs and industry groups develop and deploy grievance mechanisms for alleged human rights abuses.[19,20] The question of what rights must be protected, respected, and remediated has not been answered by the SRSG. In addressing this issue, the SRSG does recommend that careful attention be paid to the International Bill of Human Rights and the ILO core conventions because "the principles they embody comprise the benchmarks against which other social actors judge the human rights impacts of companies."

The conceptual basis for the distinction between a state *duty* to protect and a TNC *responsibility* to respect is not made clear by the SRSG, so we are left to speculate regarding the theoretical basis of the distinction. One plausible explanation is as follows: a duty invokes a moral or legal obligation, whereas a responsibility invokes accountability for praise or blame. This understanding of the distinction accurately characterizes the manner in which the SRSG parses the division of labor for protecting human rights. States, on this view, have moral and legal (or constitutional) duties to protect human rights, whereas TNCs and other business enterprises may be blamed or criticized for failing to respect human rights with possible negative consequences for the TNC. They may also be praised for respecting human rights. Such a distinction, it will be argued below, is inadequate because this framework fails to acknowledge the moral duties TNCs have to respect basic human rights.

Assessing The Tripartite Framework

Human Rights: Moral, Political, and Legal Rights

While moral rights may be used to justify some or all of international human rights law, international human rights can be justified independently of a direct correlation to morally justified human rights. More needs to be said about the substance of the human rights that the tripartite framework is intended to support and in particular the distinct human rights duties of TNCs relative to states.

It is helpful to distinguish between three conceptions of human rights: moral, political, and legal (see Figure 4.2 below). A moral or ethical

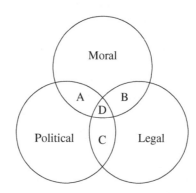

Figure 4.2   Three conceptions of rights.

conception of human rights holds that rights are ethical demands and that respecting rights is at a minimum an ethical requirement, though it may also be made a legal requirement via legitimate regulatory, judicial, and administrative mechanisms (B below).[21] Such rights are the product of careful and informed analysis and argument and are thought to be binding on all rational agents. A political conception of human rights holds that rights are political demands and that respecting such rights is at a minimum a political requirement, though it may also be a legal requirement (C below).[22] Political rights are the product of political agreements and are binding on those individuals, organizations, or nations who are party to the agreement or who are legitimately subject to those who are party to the agreement. It should be noted that political rights could also be moral rights insofar as political bodies, typically regional or international in scope, could come to agreements on human rights that were explicitly grounded in moral rights (A below). Finally, while neither moral rights nor political rights are equivalent to legal rights, moral rights that are also political rights can be made into legal rights (D below).

The human rights Norms that emerged from the Sub-Commission are an example of political conception of human rights. As stated in the preamble, the Norms are grounded in United Nations treaties and other international instruments. But as we have seen, the Sub-Commission's efforts to assign internationally recognized human rights duties to TNCs and other business enterprises based on agreements among states failed. Part of the reason the effort was unsuccessful is that the Sub-Commission made no effort to distinguish between the duties of states and the duties of TNCs. The SRSG recommends using essentially the same treaties and agreements as the grounding for the tripartite framework as the Sub-Commission did for the Norms. The main difference between these two – aside from the Framework not providing a single, integrated list of rights – is that the SRSG separates the state duty to protect from the TNC responsibility to respect. This distinction in helping to avoid the fate of the Norms merits careful attention. In the next section, I focus on the TNC responsibility to respect human rights, a feature of the tripartite framework that has received insufficient attention.

Unpacking the TNC Responsibility to Respect

To assess the distinction between the state duty to protect and the TNC duty to respect, it will be useful to examine specific human rights that are present in the treaties and agreements that the SRSG believes ground the Framework. Consider, for example, just two elements of the International Bill of Human Rights, articles 7 and 11 of the International Covenant on Economic, Social and Cultural Rights.

Article 7
The States Parties to the present Covenant recognize the right of everyone to the enjoyment of just and favourable conditions of work which ensure, in particular:

a. Remuneration which provides all workers, as a minimum, with:
   i. Fair wages and equal remuneration for work of equal value without distinction of any kind, in particular women being guaranteed conditions of work not inferior to those enjoyed by men, with equal pay for equal work;
   ii. A decent living for themselves and their families in accordance with the provisions of the present Covenant;
b. Safe and healthy working conditions;
c. Equal opportunity for everyone to be promoted in his employment to an appropriate higher level, subject to no considerations other than those of seniority and competence;
d. Rest, leisure and reasonable limitation of working hours and periodic holidays with pay, as well as remuneration for public holidays.

Article 11

1. The States Parties to the present Covenant recognize the right of everyone to an adequate standard of living for himself and his family, including adequate food, clothing and housing, and to the continuous improvement of living conditions. The States Parties will take appropriate steps to ensure the realization of this right, recognizing to this effect the essential importance of international co-operation based on free consent.
2. The States Parties to the present Covenant, recognizing the fundamental right of everyone to be free from hunger, shall take, individually and through international co-operation, the measures, including specific programmes, which are needed ... (United Nations 1966).

How is the division of responsibility for the protection of these rights to be made under the framework? On one plausible interpretation, states have a duty to put in place a regulatory framework that protects the rights articulated in these and other articles. TNCs have a responsibility to respect such regulatory frameworks by complying with all applicable law and regulations. If TNCs or other business enterprises fail to comply, then remedies need to be made available to the victims of illegal business practices.

Yet many of the states in which TNCs operate lack strong democratic legislative bodies, regulatory protection of human rights, or an adequate enforcement regime and judiciary. As the SRSG recognizes, TNCs often operate in states with weak, corrupt, or despotic regimes where there may be few national laws regulating labor practices, environmental practices, bribery, or the ownership and use of natural resources in indigenous or tribal territories. Independent of these considerations, many states simply lack the economic resources needed to implement and enforce human rights protections. In many cases, TNCs will be more readily able, within their immediate spheres of influence, to deploy the economic resources needed to avoid violating the human rights of workers and community members.

It remains unclear what the TNC responsibility to respect human rights entails in such circumstances. By way of illustration, consider two test cases that are typical of alleged human rights violations by TNCs:

1. A large US clothing retailer operates a factory in a building it leases in a Central America nation. Workers are paid the legally mandated minimum wage, but the social security wages withheld by the factory manager are not turned over to the government and credited to the workers. Wages for 48-hour work week are insufficient for subsistence so workers must put in 10–15 hours/week overtime in order to earn subsistence wages, but they are not paid legally mandated overtime wages of 50% extra per hour. Workers are occasionally forced to work 20–30 overtime hours/week in order to meet deadlines and in violation of local labor laws. Workers at the factory who are discovered to be union members are fired in violation of federal law. Government officials routinely ignore labor law violations and employees that are rumored to have filed complaints with governmental or non-governmental agencies are fired. Cutting floor workers are exposed to dangerous levels of airborne fabric particles leading to respiratory disease and there are no federal standards regarding particle exposure. Chemical shop workers are exposed to toxic chemicals resulting in neurological damage and occasional deaths.

2. In Africa, a national government licenses a Canadian mining company to develop a gold mine on land historically occupied by a tribe. Land under the control of the tribe has historically been allocated by the tribal chief, and cultivated by tribal members who in turn share their crop with the chief. In some cases tribal members grow annual crops and in other cases they grow cocoa orchards that take five to ten years to mature. The mine company has the legal authority to seize, clear, and excavate the land cultivated by farmers. Compensation is legally required, but the mining company only provides token compensation consistent with the letter of the law. The compensation does not take into account the years of work farmers have invested in cultivating the land and orchards, nor does it provide farmers with sufficient resources to acquire and develop another farm in order to cultivate food for their families and for sale or barter at market.

There are no environmental laws governing mining operations. Mine tailings contaminated with cyanide and acidic mine drainage contaminate the local rivers, killing off fish and rendering the water undrinkable and hazardous for irrigation.

The framework has similar and different implications in each case. In the first case, the government is unwilling or unable to enforce its own labor laws. It may be that it lacks the economic resources to monitor and enforce labor laws, or it may be that it believes that if it does enforce its laws TNCs will move to nations that are willing to ignore labor law violations in the interest of economic development. In addition, the legal minimum wage for workers is insufficient to ensure that the workers enjoy "a decent living for themselves and their families," and workers are forced to work in unhealthy conditions that result in respiratory disease or neurological injury over time. What does the framework's responsibility to respect human rights entail in this case? At a minimum, one would expect that respecting the human rights of workers in this case would require that local labor laws be followed by TNCs absent enforcement by authorities. But even if the TNC were to respect local labor laws, the human rights detailed above would not all be protected. Employees working a 48-hour workweek would continue to make less than subsistence wages and would be exposed to working conditions harmful to their health. The SRSG is vague about the responsibilities of TNCs in cases where nation state laws do not protect human rights. Business interests might object that taking proactive steps to protect human rights absent government regulation blurs the distinction between governments and businesses. Additionally, it might be objected that paying workers higher wages and providing a healthy working environment would unnecessarily raise the costs of production. And what of the responsibility to provide "periodic holidays with pay," which would bring additional costs? Why should TNCs voluntarily choose to bear higher costs for production?

In the second case, the mining company adheres to the minimal regulatory framework in place, but still manages to violate the farmers' right "to an adequate standard of living," including food and housing. The duty of a nation to protect human rights can reasonably be interpreted as a requirement that stronger individual property rights and environmental protection be put in place. The TNC responsibility to respect human rights might be interpreted as a willingness for mining companies to respect such regulations once they are in place, but are different actions required of the TNC by the framework independently of additional nation state regulation? Or is it the exclusive duty of the state to ensure that its citizens achieve and adequate standard of living?

Let us summarize the questions before us: (i) Why should TNCs bear higher costs in order to protect human rights, such as those described in articles 7 and

11 above, when such rights are not protected by national laws? (ii) Why should TNCs bear higher costs in order to respect human rights in states that do not make a concerted effort to enforce their own laws?

On a political conception of human rights, duties are derived from political agreements and are binding on those organizations or nations who are party to the agreement or who are legitimately subject to those who are party to the agreement. The answer to question 1, from the political perspective, is that TNCs should respect human rights when doing so will result in higher costs if they were party to the original agreement, or if they later endorsed the agreement. For example, if a TNC, or its appointed representative, participated in the process that produced the agreement stipulating the duties of TNCs it would be bound by the agreement. Or, if the TNC did not participate in the creation of the original agreement, but subsequently endorsed the agreement, the TNC would be bound by the duties of the agreement. For example, while TNCs were not formal parties to the creation of the Global Compact, they could become bound by its principles by endorsing the compact. TNCs not party to the original agreement, or who did not subsequently endorse the agreement, would not be bound by the human rights duties articulated in the agreement and one would have no claim against them in jurisdictions with little or no protection of the rights of workers.

The answer to question 2 is similar to the answer in question 1 on a political conception of human rights duties. In cases where host nations make little or no effort to enforce laws that protect basic human rights, TNCs should respect human rights laws if they were party to the original agreement, or if they later endorse the agreement. TNCs not party to the original agreement, or who did not subsequently endorse the agreement, would have no basis for respecting laws that are not respected and enforced by the host nation.

We asked why TNCs should bear higher costs in order to protect human rights, such as those described in articles 7 and 11 above, when such rights are not protected by national laws. We also asked why TNCs should bear higher costs in order to respect human rights in states that do not enforce their own laws. The answer is the same in both cases. On the political conception of human rights, TNCs that are not legitimately bound by the Framework and that have no instrumental reasons for adhering to elements of the Framework, have no reasons for respecting laws that protect human rights when they could lawfully do otherwise, and they have no reason for adhering to unenforced laws within states barring independent considerations. What independent considerations are relevant here?

The primary independent considerations are strategic one's concerning corporate reputation. For example, if TNCs incur negative publicity harmful to brand reputation for acting illegally it would have instrumental reasons for respecting host nation labor laws that are independent of political duties regarding human rights. That is, TNCs that wished to protect brand identity from targeted criticism by NGOs for legal violations have independent reasons for adhering to unenforced host nation labor laws.[23]

Three features of a purely strategic attitude toward human rights should be noted. First, companies that do not have widely recognized brands that render them vulnerable to NGO pressure have little or no strategic reasons for respecting human rights. In such cases, the risk of negative publicity as a result of NGO activity is so small that the added costs of respecting articles 7 and 11 will not be justified on strategic grounds. Second, companies that employ a purely strategic attitude toward human rights, and who do not fear NGO criticism, may utilize any labor practices permitted by local governments whether these are lawful or not in the host nation. For example, forced labor may be utilized as a low or zero cost labor source. Third, for NGO criticism to be persuasive in civil society, it must be grounded in widely acknowledged moral prescriptions. Without such grounding, NGOs are unlikely to persuade consumers, shareholders, and others that a TNC is engaged in activity that should be criticized or condemned. NGOs that can appeal to basic moral norms when criticizing TNCs may be able to bring to bear greater pressure and cause more harm to TNC reputations than NGOs whose criticism is not grounded in basic moral norms. This is because basic moral norms are less contentious and more widely shared than are other moral demands. For example, NGOs that criticize the use of forced labor or practices that unnecessarily put workers' physical welfare at risk (e.g., through poor maintenance of machinery) are likely to garner more support from a wider range of individuals than NGOs that criticize a company's failure to provide "the highest attainable standard of physical and mental health."

On a moral or ethical conception human rights duties are derived from ethical norms that are binding on all agents. Previous efforts to articulate human rights duties for TNCs, such as the UN Norms, failed in part because they were unable to differentiate between basic rights, such as the liberty to seek out favorable employment, that should always be protected, and aspirational rights, such as "the highest attainable standard of physical and mental health," that states might identify as worthy goals once basic rights have been widely secured. This chapter defends the view that TNCs have ethically grounded basic human rights duties that should be incorporated into the tripartite framework, and that these perfect duties are distinct from any imperfect duties TNCs may have regarding aspirational rights.[24] In this view, TNCs must meet basic human rights obligations in all of their operations regardless of whether such duties are recognized by host nation laws or whether host nations enforce such laws, because they are comprised of agents on whom human rights duties are binding. On this conception of human rights, meeting human rights duties is to be understood as a necessary cost of doing business. The final part of this chapter defends an account of the moral duties of TNCs with respect to basic human rights.

Corporate Duties

There is widespread agreement that there are at least some morally grounded rights that TNCs and other businesses have a duty to respect, and not merely among NGO representatives and the drafters of the UN Norms. Businesses and trade groups also routinely express a moral commitment to respect human rights. For example, the Business Leaders Initiative on Human Rights states that it "strongly supports respect for human rights ... *because it is the right thing to do*."[25] There can be little doubt that among the reasons that companies sign the Global Compact is the view that there are human rights that businesses have a moral duty to respect. For example, Novartis, both an early signatory of the Global Compact and a founder of the BLIHR, holds that "Human rights apply to all people throughout the world. They should guarantee everyone, everywhere, a life in freedom and dignity."[26] The BLIHR (2009) itself endorses a role for business in promoting a new social and international order in which human rights are protected and respected.[27] However, while there may be agreement among many international actors that certain rights must be respected by TNCs in their global operations whether or not those rights are protected by nation states, there does not appear to be agreement on the content of those rights.

If one grants that basic rights to liberty, physical security, and subsistence, physical security, and subsistence have been established, further precision is required.[28] In particular, the specific duties entailed by these rights need to be articulated in the context of TNC relationships between workers, community members, and others. Here it will be useful to return to our examples and explain the implications of a moral account of human rights for understanding the duties of TNCs in those specific cases. Let us recall the questions we asked previously: (i) Why should TNCs bear higher costs in order to protect human rights, such as those described in articles 7 and 11 of the International Covenant on Economic, Social and Cultural Rights, when such rights are not protected by national laws? (ii) Why should TNCs bear higher costs in order to respect human rights in states that do not make a concerted effort to enforce their own laws?

The answer to question 1, from the perspective of an agentically grounded account of human rights, is that TNCs have a perfect duty to respect basic human rights even when doing so will result in higher costs. In the example of the Central American factory, let us note that the workers must spend a specified number of hours in the factory as a condition of employment. Second, let us acknowledge that workers are vulnerable to injury or death at work from poor maintenance, poor or non-existent safety equipment, and exposure to dangerous chemicals. On the view defended here, workers have a legitimate claim right to have their physical health protected while at work and TNCs have a duty to take proactive measures to protect the health of workers. TNC duties include ensuring the physical security of employees by educating them about workplace hazards on the cutting floor and in the chemical shop and providing the safety equipment necessary for employees to protect their health. TNC duties also include respecting the workers' right to liberty by refraining from forcing workers to work overtime and by permitting union activity. And TNC duties require respecting the right to subsistence by ensuring that employees are paid wages for a standard work-week that allows them to purchase those goods (e.g., food, shelter, transportation, and other basic necessities) necessary for normal human functioning. While it is difficult to establish a universal wage standard compatible with the right to subsistence, it is possible to identify subsistence wage formulas that provide managers with the necessary practical guidance. More comprehensive efforts to identify the duties of TNCs to workers in global supply chains are provided in Chapter 5.

In the African mining case, TNC duties include respecting the farmers' right to subsistence by fairly compensating them for their farms so that they have the resources necessary to start new farms elsewhere. Respecting the right to subsistence also requires ensuring either that the local water supply continues to be sufficiently pollution free, so that it may be used for irrigation, drinking water, and fishing, or that an alternative water supply suitable for these purpose is made available.

The answer to question 2 is similar to the answer in question 1 on the moral conception of human rights duties defended here. In cases where host nations make little or no effort to enforce labor and other laws that protect basic human rights, TNCs should respect such laws in recognition of their basic human rights duties. There is a second moral reason as well, one that it is independent of the basic duty to respect human rights. TNCs that fail to respect local labor laws violate the moral principle of fair play. When operating in nations with weak legal enforcement of labor laws, TNCs nonetheless expect their own legal rights regarding private property ownership, taxation, and contracts, for example to be vigorously enforced and typically exert economic, political, and legal pressure to ensure such protection. Circumstances such as this, H.L.A. Hart argues, create special rights and duties independent of other moral considerations. Hart refers to this source of obligations as "mutuality of restrictions" and describes it as follows: "when a number of persons conduct any joint enterprise according to rules and thus restrict their liberty, those who have submitted to these restrictions when required have a right to a similar submission from those who have benefited by their submission."[29] Economic activity is always a joint enterprise and TNCs and their agents incur obligations of reciprocity by virtue of their participation in economic activity and the attendant regulatory framework. In this case, the utilization of the legal framework of host nations entails a reciprocal obligation on the part of TNCs to respect local labor and environmental laws, and a moral claim right of host-nation workers and community members against TNCs to respect their legal rights.[30]

If TNCs do have perfect duties grounded in an agentic conception of human rights, as has been argued in Chapter 3, then we need to ask whether this view is compatible with the tripartite framework of the SRSG. The view defended here should be regarded as compatible with the framework while providing a more definitive, universally binding basis for TNC human rights duties. The call for TNCs to respect basic human rights is not merely grounded in a strategically appropriate response to civil society organizations, it is an ethical duty for all TNC managers executives and directors. Moral arguments for TNC human rights duties in no way undermine the importance of state duties to protect human rights. Indeed, a realistic assessment of current global business practices demonstrates a need for both strong state human rights protections and strong global institutions to combat human rights abuses (Hsieh 2009, pp. 251–273; Kobrin 2009, pp. 349–374; Wettstein 2010, pp. 275–283). But to rephrase the SRSG, the human rights regime rests upon the bedrock moral duty of all agents and institutions to respect basic human rights.[31]

Are Human Rights Merely a Western Idea?

At this point in our analysis, it is worthwhile to consider an objection to the foregoing argument concerning human rights. This criticism stems from the observation that the idea of human rights emerged from the Western philosophical tradition, but is taken to be universal in its applicability. In liberal market economies, such as the United States, the United Kingdom, and Australia, the moral tradition of liberalism predominates. This tradition emphasizes individual liberty and the equality of persons by enfranchising the protection of a variety of economic and social rights and democratic political control (Donnelly 2003, pp. 48–49). Critics claim that human rights are of less importance in the value systems of other cultures and other economic systems. For example, it is argued that "Asian values" emphasize order, discipline, and social harmony, as opposed to individual rights. In this view, the basic rights of individuals should not be allowed to interfere with the harmony of the community, as might be the case, for example when workers engage in disruptive collective action in an effort to secure their rights. This view might also be used to defend the claim that the moral norms that govern Asian factory operations should emphasize order and discipline, not basic rights.

Several points may be made in reply to this objection. First, Asia is a large region with a vast and heterogeneous population. As Amartya Sen and others have argued, to claim that all, or even most, Asians share a uniform set of values is to impose a level of uniformity that does not exist at present and has not existed in the past (Donnely 1999; Sen 1999, 2000; Tatsuo 1999). Second, in secular, democratic Asian societies such as India, respect for individual rights has a long tradition. Indeed, there are significant antecedents in the history of the civilizations of the Indian subcontinent that emphasize the equivalent of basic rights. For example, in the third century BC, the Emperor Ashoka granted his citizens the freedom to embrace whatever religious or philosophical system they might choose, while he emphasized the importance of tolerance and respect for philosophical and religious beliefs different than one's own (Sen 1999). Third, even if it was the case that Asian cultures shared a uniform set of values that de-emphasized human rights, this would not by itself provide good reasons for denying or disrespecting basic rights. This is because the justification of human rights provided above is grounded in rational arguments that are valid across cultures. The critic is likely to retort that such a view reflects Western prejudices grounded in Enlightenment ideals. This response is unpersuasive. Diverse intellectual traditions have emphasized the importance of values derived from reason, rather than mythology, traditionalism, mere sentiment, or some other source.

Consider the case of China, where Confucianism is the predominate moral tradition. This tradition emphasizes relationships between people, including duties to family and to other members of one's community. Here, the emphasis is on the cultivation of virtue, including *ren* understood as caring for others. While the concept of rights is not a part of classical Confucianism, it is compatible with contemporary Confucianism. As Joseph Chan has argued, human rights may be regarded as a safety net in place when ren is insufficient for ensuring that individuals are properly cared for "the Confucian perspective would take rights as a fallback auxiliary apparatus that serves to protect basic human interests in case virtues do not obtain or human relationships clearly break down" (Chan 1999, p. 228). This will be especially true of the basic rights necessary for human flourishing such as subsistence. While the justification of rights is different, there is good reason for thinking that most of the basic rights enfranchised in the new international human rights regimes are justifiable on Confucian grounds, as well as liberal grounds. The main point of this observation is that ethical norms of one of China's main ethical tradition are consistent with important elements of the international human rights regime. Significantly, the Chinese government itself has in recent years endorsed the universality of human rights, although hedging to a certain extent when claiming that it is "natural" for nations to differ on human rights issues depending on factors such as their level of development, history, and culture (Sceates and Breslin 2012, p. 8).

Consistent with the analysis of the UN SRSG, there are also pragmatic reasons that non-Western cultures may seek to embrace the international human rights regime. Chinese companies, including state-owned enterprises, operating in foreign markets face legitimacy problems that negatively impact their reputation, undermine their stakeholder relationships, and result in negative business outcomes. For example, China Non-Ferrous Metals Mining Corporation has been accused of systematic and widespread labor rights violations in its Zambian mines. Human Rights Watch issued a 122-page report targeted at institutional investors and intended to diminish demand for CNMC's initial public offering in Hong Kong (Human Rights Watch 2011). Companies may seek to gain legitimacy by CSR practices consistent with the local environments in which they operate (Yang and Rivers 2009). However, host nation standards vary widely and in many cases diverge from established international norms regarding human rights (Donaldson 1991; United Nations Special Representative 2008). Chinese companies have been criticized for operating in pariah states that engage in systematic human rights abuses such as North Korea, Mynmar, and Zimbabwe (Shankleman 2009) and for a poor record of CSR, especially in Africa, including "having a damaging impact in terms of environmental degradation, working conditions, displacement of local communities, corruption, and fiscal evasion" (Shelton and Kabemba 2012, pp. 231–232). In general, Chinese companies have as a group made fewer public commitments to adhere to human rights than have Western companies (Ruggie 2008).

The primary reason that companies based in LMEs have made commitments to human rights initiatives, such as the UN Global Compact, has been the pressure applied by nongovernmental organizations (Clapham 2006, Joseph 2004; Rodman 1998). This pressure has included boycotts, publicity campaigns, investor activism, litigation by human rights advocacy groups, and negotiations undertaken by multilateral organizations such as the World Bank, International Monetary Fund, and the OECD. The primary institutional pressure applied to Chinese corporations is that of the Chinese government (more accurately, specific elements of the government such as the Ministry of Foreign Affairs, the Ministry of Commerce, and the state-owned Assets Supervision and Administration Commission). Current Chinese government priorities with respect to overseas development are FDI and the acquisition of hydrocarbons and other natural resources such as wood, copper and rare earth elements (Kaplinsky et al. 2007). Social and environmental responsibility initiatives, including international human rights standards, are not presently a priority. However, to the extent that Chinese TNCs confront legitimacy problems regarding their social license to operate in important geopolitical regions such as Africa, embracing and enacting human rights standards, such as those articulated in the *Guiding Principles*, can make them more competitive with TNCs that presently utilize human rights standards in their global operations. It is also likely to provide them with greater legitimacy and political support in developing nations that are at least partially free and enjoy at least some political rights and civil liberties. Given the historical record of many Western TNCs operating in developing nations, there is a distinct opportunity for firms from rapidly growing economies to learn from history and implement best practices regarding human rights in their global operations.

Conclusion

This chapter has examined the recent history of UN initiatives regarding business and human rights and placed the "'Protect, Respect and Remedy' Framework for Business and Human Rights" and its accompanying *Guiding Principles on Business and Human Rights* in an historical context. It has been argued that the tripartite framework's grounding of the responsibility of TNCs to respect human rights is properly understood as a moral and not merely as a political or legal duty. A moral account of the duty of TNCs to respect basic human rights has been defended and contrasted with a merely strategic approach. The main conclusion of the chapter is that only a moral account of the basic human rights duties of transnational companies provides a sufficiently deep justification of "the corporate responsibility to respect human rights" feature of the tripartite framework. The next three chapters apply the cosmopolitan human rights framework to practical problems in international business.

A. Appendix

Norms on the Responsibilities of Transnational Corporations and Other Business Enterprises with Regard to Human Rights

A. **General Obligations**
   1. States have the primary responsibility to promote, secure the fulfilment of, respect, ensure respect of, and protect human rights recognised in international as well as national law, including assuring that transnational corporations and other business enterprises respect human rights. Within their respective spheres of activity and influence, transnational corporations and other business enterprises have the obligation to promote, secure the fulfilment of, respect, ensure respect of, and protect human rights recognized in international as well as national law.

B. **Right to Equal Opportunity and Nondiscriminatory Treatment**

2. Transnational corporations and other business enterprises shall ensure equality of opportunity and treatment, as provided in the relevant international instruments and national legislation as well as international human rights law, for the purpose of eliminating discrimination based on race, color, sex, language, religion, political opinion, national or social origin, social status, indigenous status, disability, age (except for children who may be given greater protection), or other status of the individual unrelated to the inherent requirements to perform the job, or complying with special measures designed to overcome past discrimination against certain groups.

C. **Right to Security of Persons**

3. Transnational corporations and other business enterprises shall not engage in nor benefit from war crimes; crimes against humanity; genocide; torture; forced disappearance; forced or compulsory labor; hostage-taking; extrajudicial, summary or arbitrary executions; other violations of humanitarian law; and other international crimes against the human person as defined by international law, in particular human rights and humanitarian law.

4. Security arrangements for transnational corporations and other business enterprises shall observe international human rights norms as well as the laws and professional standards of the country or countries in which they operate.

D. **Rights of Workers**

5. Transnational corporations and other business enterprises shall not use forced or compulsory labor as forbidden by the relevant international instruments and national legislation, as well as international human rights and humanitarian law.

6. Transnational corporations and other business enterprises shall respect the rights of children to be protected from economic exploitation as forbidden by the relevant international instruments and national legislation as well as international human rights and humanitarian law.

7. Transnational corporations and other business enterprises shall provide a safe and healthy working environment as set forth in relevant international instruments and national legislation as well as international human rights and humanitarian law.

8. Transnational corporations and other business enterprises shall provide workers with remuneration that ensures an adequate standard of living for them and their families. Such remuneration shall take due account of their needs for adequate living conditions with a view toward progressive improvement.

9. Transnational corporations and other business enterprises shall ensure the freedom of association and effective recognition of the right to collective bargaining by protecting the right to establish and, subject only to the rules of the organization concerned, to join organizations of their own choosing without distinction, previous authorization, or interference, for the protection of their employment interests and for other collective bargaining purposes as provided in national legislation and the relevant ILO conventions.

E. **Respect for National Sovereignty and Human Rights**

10. Transnational corporations and other business enterprises shall recognize and respect applicable norms of international law; national laws; regulations; administrative practices; the rule of law; the public interest; development objectives; social, economic, and cultural policies including transparency, accountability, and prohibition of corruption; and authority of the countries in which the enterprises operate.

11. Transnational corporations and other business enterprises shall not offer, promise, give, accept, condone, knowingly benefit from, or demand a bribe or other improper advantage. Nor shall they be solicited or expected to give a bribe or other improper advantage to any government, public official, candidate for elective post, any member of the armed forces or security forces, or any other individual or organization. Transnational corporations and other business enterprises shall refrain from any activity which supports, solicits, or encourages States or any other entities to abuse human rights. They shall further seek to ensure that the goods and services they provide will not be used to abuse human rights.

12. Transnational corporations and other business enterprises shall respect civil, cultural, economic, political, and social rights, and contribute to their realization, in particular the rights to development; adequate food and drinking water; the highest attainable standard of physical and mental health; adequate housing; privacy; education; freedom of thought, conscience, and religion; and freedom of opinion and expression; and refrain from actions which obstruct or impede the realization of those rights.

F. **Obligations with Regard to Consumer Protection**

13. Transnational corporations and other business enterprises shall act in accordance with fair business, marketing, and advertising practices and shall take all necessary steps to ensure the safety and quality of the goods and services they provide, including observance of the precautionary principle. Nor shall they produce, distribute, market, or advertise potentially harmful or harmful products for use by consumers.

G. **Obligations with Regard to Environmental Protection**
   14. Transnational corporations and other business enterprises shall carry out their activities in accordance with national laws, regulations, administrative practices, and policies relating to the preservation of the environment of the countries in which they operate, as well as in accordance with relevant international agreements, principles, objectives, responsibilities, and standards with regard to the environment, as well as human rights, public health and safety, bioethics, and the precautionary principle; and shall generally conduct their activities in a manner contributing to the wider goal of sustainable development.

H. **General Provisions of Implementation**
   15. As an initial step toward implementing these Norms each transnational corporation or other business enterprise shall adopt, disseminate, and implement internal rules of operation in compliance with the Norms. Further, they shall periodically report on and take other measures fully to implement the Norms and to provide at least for the prompt implementation of the protections set forth in the Norms. Each transnational corporation or other business enterprise shall apply and incorporate these Norms in their contracts or other arrangements and dealings with contractors, subcontractors, suppliers, licensees, distributors, or natural or other legal persons that enter into any agreement with the transnational corporation or business enterprise in order to ensure respect for and implementation of the Norms.

   16. Transnational corporations and other businesses enterprises shall be subject to periodic monitoring and verification by United Nations, other international, and national mechanisms, already in existence or yet to be created, regarding application of the Norms. This monitoring shall be transparent, independent, and take into account input from stakeholders (including NGOs) and as a result of complaints of violations of these Norms. Further, transnational corporations and other businesses enterprises shall conduct periodic evaluations concerning the impact of their own activities on human rights under these Norms.

   17. States should establish and reinforce the necessary legal and administrative framework for assuring that the Norms and other relevant national and international laws are implemented by transnational corporations and other business enterprises.

   18. Transnational corporations and other business enterprises shall provide prompt, effective, and adequate reparation to those persons, entities, and communities that have been adversely affected by failures to

comply with these Norms through, *inter alia*, reparations, restitution, compensation, and rehabilitation for any damage done or property taken. In connection with determining damages, and in all other respects, these Norms shall be enforced by national courts and/or international tribunals if appropriate.

19. Nothing in these Norms shall be construed as diminishing, restricting, or adversely affecting the human rights obligations of States under national and international law. Nor shall they be construed as diminishing, restricting, or adversely affecting more protective human rights norms. Nor shall they be construed as diminishing, restricting, or adversely affecting other obligations or responsibilities of transnational corporations and other business enterprises in fields other than human rights.

I. Definitions

20. The term "transnational corporation" refers to an economic entity operating in more than one country or a cluster of economic entities operating in two or more countries – whatever their legal form, whether in their home country or country of activity, and whether taken individually or collectively.

21. The phrase "other business enterprise" includes any business entity, regardless of the international or domestic nature of its activities, including a transnational corporation; the corporate, partnership, or other legal form used to establish the business entity; and the nature of the ownership of the entity. These Norms shall be presumed to apply, as a matter of practice, if the business enterprise has any relation with a transnational corporation, the impact of its activities is not entirely local, or the activities involve violations of the right to security as indicated in paragraphs three and four.

22. The term "stakeholder" includes stockholders, other owners, workers, and their representatives, as well as any other individual or group that is affected by the activities of transnational corporations or other business enterprises. The term "stakeholder" shall be interpreted functionally in light of the objectives of these Norms and include indirect stakeholders when their interests are or will be substantially affected by the activities of the transnational corporation or business enterprise. In addition to parties directly affected by the activities of business enterprises, stakeholders can include parties which are indirectly affected by the activities of transnational corporations or other business enterprises such as consumer groups, customers, governments, neighbouring communities, indigenous peoples and communities, NGOs, public and private lending institutions, suppliers, trade associations, and others.

23. The phrases "internationally recognized human rights" and "international human rights" include civil, cultural, economic, political, and social rights, as set forth in the International Bill of Human Rights and other human rights treaties, as well as the right to development and rights recognized by international humanitarian law, international refugee law, international labor law, and other relevant instruments adopted within the United Nations system (United Nations 2003).[32]

Notes

1. United Nations Special Representative of the Secretary General on the Issue of Human Rights and Transnational Corporations and Other Business Enterprises (2006).
2. United Nations Commission on Human Rights (2005).
3. United Nations Special Representative of the Secretary General on the Issue of Human Rights and Transnational Corporations and Other Business Enterprises (2008).
4. United Nations Global Compact, *UN Global Compact Participants*. URL = http://www.unglobalcompact.org/ParticipantsAndStakeholders/index.html.
5. International Chamber of Commerce and the International Organisation of Employers (2003); United States Council for International Business (undated).
6. The positive argument for human rights duties is made in part III of this essay. O'Neill's views on the obligations of TNCs regarding global justice are spelled out in her essay (O'Neill 2001).
7. The complete mandate is as follows: (i) To identify and clarify standards of corporate responsibility and accountability for transnational corporations and other business enterprises with regard to human rights; (ii) To elaborate on the role of States in effectively regulating and adjudicating the role of transnational corporations and other business enterprises with regard to human rights, including through international cooperation; (iii) To research and clarify the implications for transnational corporations and other business enterprises of concepts such as "complicity" and "sphere of influence"; (iv) To develop materials and methodologies for undertaking human rights impact assessments of the activities of transnational corporations and other business enterprises; (v) To compile a compendium of best practices of States and transnational corporations and other business enterprises" (United Nations Commission on Human Rights 2005).
8. United Nations Special Representative of the Secretary General on the Issue of Human Rights and Transnational Corporations and Other Business Enterprises (2006).
9. United Nations Special Representative of the Secretary General on the Issue of Human Rights and Transnational Corporations and Other Business Enterprises (2008).
10. The United Nations 'Protect, Respect and Remedy' Framework, summarized by the *Guiding Principles*, was developed by the Special Representative of the

Secretary-General on the issue of human rights and transnational corporations and other business enterprises and endorsed by the Human Rights Council in its resolution 17/4 of June 16, 2011.

11. United Nations Special Representative of the Secretary General on the Issue of Human Rights and Transnational Corporations and Other Business Enterprises (2006, p. 14).

12. United Nations Special Representative of the Secretary General on the Issue of Human Rights and Transnational Corporations and Other Business Enterprises (2006, pp. 10–14).

13. United Nations Special Representative of the Secretary General on the Issue of Human Rights and Transnational Corporations and Other Business Enterprises (2006, p. 16).

14. United Nations Special Representative of the Secretary General on the Issue of Human Rights and Transnational Corporations and Other Business Enterprises (2006, pp. 17–20).

15. United Nations Special Representative of the Secretary General on the Issue of Human Rights and Transnational Corporations and Other Business Enterprises (2006, p. 16).

16. United Nations Special Representative of the Secretary General on the Issue of Human Rights and Transnational Corporations and Other Business Enterprises (2006, p. 17).

17. United Nations Special Representative of the Secretary General on the Issue of Human Rights and Transnational Corporations and Other Business Enterprises (2006, p. 17).

18. United Nations Special Representative of the Secretary General on the Issue of Human Rights and Transnational Corporations and Other Business Enterprises (2006, p. 22).

19. Buchanan provides a compelling argument for the conclusion that the international legal system of human rights can be provided with a robust, pluralistic moral justification (that includes, among many other elements, the normative justification of the institutions and practices that create the system). Buchanan, A.E. (2009). *Human Rights, Legitimacy, and the Use of Force*. New York: Oxford University Press; Buchanan (2013), note 29, 14–22.

20. United Nations Special Representative of the Secretary General on the Issue of Human Rights and Transnational Corporations and Other Business Enterprises (2006, pp. 24–25).

21. For a recent defense of this position see (Sen 2004).

22. For example, James Nickel reports that "Human rights are political norms dealing mainly with how people should be treated by their governments and institutions." (Nickel 2009).

23. United Nations Special Representative of the Secretary General on the Issue of Human Rights and Transnational Corporations and Other Business Enterprises (2006, pp. 16–24).

24. Perfect duties admit of no exception, whereas imperfect duties may be fulfilled on ocassion and at the discretion of the duty bearer. The locus classicus is (Kant 1990; Thompson 1993; Zimmerman 1996).

25. United States Council for International Business (undated); Business Leaders Initiative on Human Rights (2009).
26. Novartis, "Human Rights," URL = <http://www.corporatecitizenship.novartis.com/people-communities/human-rights.shtml>.
27. Business Leaders Initiative on Human Rights (2009).
28. I do not mean to imply that this is the only conceivable list of basic human rights, but rather that it is plausible account that has stood the test of time and philosophical scrutiny well.
29. (Hart, 1955: 175-191, 185).
30. The complex issue of responsibility for the labor practices of contractors is beyond the scope of this essay. For discussion see (Arnold and Bowie 2003, pp. 225–227; Arnold and Bowie 2007, pp. 135–145, 136–138).
31. Legitimate skepticism about the role of rights in the workplace might nonetheless be voiced by managers and others in nations where human rights discourse is foreign. For recent discussion of this issue, see (Michaelson 2010, pp. 237–251; Strudler 2008, pp. 67–84).
32. Sub-Commission on Protection & Promotion of Human Rights, Working Group, *Norms on the Responsibilities of Transnational Corporations and Other Business Enterprises with Regard to Human Rights.*

Chapter Five

On the Division of Moral Labor for Human Rights Between States and Corporations

Status Egalitarianism and State Obligations

Harvard Professor Nieh-hê Hsieh has argued that corporations should not be understood to have human rights obligations because, as private actors, corporations are not the proper type of institutions to protect status egalitarianism in society (Hsieh 2015). Hsieh argues that "if we take as central to human rights the ideal of *status egalitarianism*, then there is reason to reject assigning human rights obligations to MNEs and their managers" (Hsieh 2015, 219). His discussion of status egalitarianism, or the equal standing of citizens, is derivative of the work of Allen Buchanan whose explicit focus is the international legal human rights system. Buchanan characterizes status egalitarianism as "*a robust commitment to affirming and protecting the equal basic moral status of all individuals*" and he quite reasonably argues that status egalitarianism is an important "aspect" of the international legal human rights system (Buchanan 2013, 27, 29–30).

Hsieh argues that TNCs do not have human rights obligations for two reasons. First, "to assign human rights obligations to MNEs is to ask them to adopt a perspective of impartiality and equal treatment that seems not only overly demanding but also incompatible with what is required of private actors in the realm of economic activity" (Hsieh 2015, 226). Hsieh does not argue for this claim or explain why impartiality and equal treatment of, say, customers or employees is incompatible with economic activity. Second, Hsieh claims that status egalitarianism needs to be enforced by "institutions at the level of society" and that "by placing human rights obligations on [TNCs], in a sense the scope of status equality shrinks. That is, no longer are citizens understood to be members in equal standing in relation to one another but rather in equal

The Ethics of Global Business, First Edition. Denis G. Arnold.
© 2023 John Wiley & Sons Ltd. Published 2023 by John Wiley & Sons Ltd.

standing in relation to others within the scope of activity of [TNCs]" (Hsieh 2015, 226). Again, the argument is not precisely clear. Hsieh moves from the plausible claim that societal institutions are required to support status egalitarianism to the puzzling conclusion that when TNCs support the enforcement and protection of human rights standards, status equality "shrinks." Let us consider these claims in succession.

Are Economic Actors Exempt from Human Rights Obligations?

Hsieh claims that obligations of impartiality and equal treatment are incompatible with the economic activity of corporations. There are at least two ways of interpreting this claim. First, it might be interpreted as maintaining that firms do not have this obligation with respect to their employees, customers, and others with whom they interact because it is incompatible with the economic function of business. On this reading, Hsieh would seem to be committed to the position that TNCs have no obligation to avoid discrimination. For example, on this interpretation, firms should be free to discriminate in hiring based on race, sex, or caste, they should be free to discriminate against women by paying men more than women for equal work, and they should be free to discriminate against the poor by requiring them to work overtime to earn subsistence wages and by neglecting their health and safety at work. Perhaps, Hsieh would argue that this is only the case when it is lawful to do so; however, it remains unclear why the legal prohibition would constitute a reason for firms to refrain from discrimination if as economic actors they are not obligated to respect the protection of human rights by states as outlined in the *Guiding Principles*. In other words, Hsieh seems committed to the position that as economic actors, firms have no obligations other than to maximize economic value. Hsieh does not explicitly embrace the shareholder primacy view and instrumental corporate responsibility, but it is difficult to understand how this position can be defended absent an appeal to some version of the shareholder primacy ideology. Nor is it clear how Hsieh would respond to the arguments discussed previously in this book that have claimed direct, moral human rights obligations on the part of TNCs.

Alternatively, Hsieh might be read as claiming that TNCs have no obligations to promote and protect status egalitarian values and practices in society at large. On this interpretation, Hsieh is interpreted as maintaining that TNCs should not be asked to take on a role analogous to nation states in ensuring that status egalitarian ideas are promoted and protected for all people globally. For example, TNCs should not be expected to ensure that all members of society meet basic social welfare standards. If this interpretation is correct, it is a puzzling criticism of corporate human rights obligations (both agentically grounded human rights obligations and obligations grounded in the work of the UN and ILO). The *Guiding Principles*, for example, were carefully designed specifically to avoid confusion about the roles of corporations versus states in the promotion and protection of human rights. More specifically, the *Guiding Principles* recognize: "The role of business enterprises as specialized organs of society performing specialized functions, required to comply with all applicable laws and to respect human rights" (Human Rights Council 2011: 1). The *Guiding Principles* require that firms, "Avoid causing or contributing to adverse human rights impacts *through their own activities*, and address such impacts when they occur" and "Seek to prevent or mitigate adverse human rights impacts that are *directly linked to their operations, products or services by their business relationships*, even if they have not contributed to those impacts" (Human Rights Council 2011: 15). There is no expectation that TNCs and other business enterprises take on a state-like role regarding human rights in the United Nations "Protect, Respect and Remedy" framework. It is true that some theorists defend a state-like role for corporations that is constrained only by the capacities of the firm (Wettstein 2009), but that is neither the view articulated by the *Guiding Principles* nor by most scholars who have defended corporate human rights obligations (Bishop 2012; Cragg 2004, 2009; Donaldson 1991; Kobrin 2009). It is certainly not a position advocated in this work.

Do TNC Human Rights Obligations "Shrink" Equal Standing Among Persons?

Hsieh's second claim is that when TNCs and other business enterprises fulfill human rights obligations, "status equality shrinks." By this he appears to mean that by fulfilling human rights obligations, TNCs diminish the standing of equality in society. But why should this be the case? No defenders of corporate human rights obligations maintain that TNCs and other business enterprises ought to supersede the role of the state in the promotion and protection of human rights, including those most closely linked to status egalitarianism. The "worry" as expressed by Hsieh may have its most plausible articulation when applied to TNCs operating in nations where governance gaps are the most grievous. Under those circumstances, the states fail to meet the expectations of the international legal human rights system with respect to the protection of status equality for its citizens. Hsieh's argument appears to be that if TNCs attempt to protect status equality in their spheres of influence, they will diminish the standing of status equality beyond their sphere of influence. How should theorists and proponents of corporate human rights obligations respond?

Let us begin by noting that even under such circumstances, the expectation is not that TNCs ensure status equality for everyone or even status equality for those directly impacted by their operations, but instead the expectation is that they meet a more limited scope of obligations. In the international legal human rights system that is the focus of Buchanan's analysis (and hence Hsieh's), the explicit expectation of TNCs is that they "avoid infringing on the human rights of others" and "address adverse human rights impacts with which they are involved" (Human Rights Council 2011: 13). In governance voids, where human rights are not protected by the state, status equality and respect for human rights more generally are already greatly diminished. If TNCs operating in such governance voids meet human rights obligations (e.g. the ILO conventions), doing so will *enhance* rather than diminish status equality, as it will expand the extent to which human rights are respected. Hsieh's position appears wedded to the old model of an individual–State dichotomy, and resistant to the multi-actor system associated with the emergence of a transnational world order populated by supranational organizations that is the basis of the new corporate human rights agenda. Indeed, Hsieh's position is inconsistent with that of Buchanan, whose conclusions regarding the current international legal human rights system include the idea that "In principle, there appears to be no barrier to modifying the system of international legal human rights" to hold "non-state actors such as global corporations" legally accountable for human rights duties articulated in the *Guiding Principles* (Buchanan 2013, 284).

The current multi-actor international system requires a different conceptualization of the moral division of labor than has been favored by political philosophers historically. Typically, political philosophers have defended a conception of the basic structure of society between governments and individuals. Rawls' theory of justice includes a prototypical example of this dualist conception of the basic structure of society (Rawls 1999, 268–269). From a Rawlsian perspective, corporations are mere associations of individuals like church congregations, local sports clubs, and book clubs.[1] Hsieh's scholarship has focused on the application of Rawlsian political philosophy to problems in business ethics, so it is not surprising that he would embrace the same division of moral labor in society (Hsieh 2004, 2009). An alternative conceptualization of the division of moral labor is needed for the existing multi-actor international economic, legal, and political system. TNCs should be conceptualized not as mere associations of individuals, but as organizations distinct from governments, willing and capable of exerting significant influence over governments but typically with allegiance to no government. Cragg has persuasively argued that while TNCs have human rights obligations in the international system for similar reasons to nation states, this does not entail that they have the same human rights obligations (Cragg 2009). TNCs have

---

[1] For a critique of this conception of the basic structure of society, see Chapter Two. For a general critique of the use of Rawlsian theory in business ethics scholarship, see Norman (2015) and Singer (2015).

direct and indirect impacts on the human rights of individuals wherever they operate. In a pluralistic account of the international system, TNCs are properly and legitimately held accountable for these impacts. Indeed, the primary way that firms can gain normative legitimacy when operating in nations with significant governance gaps is by meeting human rights obligations in their operations (Cragg 2009; Donaldson 1991). By advocating a dualist basic structure for the international system, one in which corporations have no direct or indirect human rights obligations, Hsieh is arguing for a Westphalian model in a post-Westphalian era (Kobrin 2009, Santoro 2010).

The Post-Westphalian International Order

One distinctive feature of the post-Westphalian international order is the significant increase in the influence and power of corporations throughout the world and the inability on the part of many governments to constrain corporate operations that directly or indirectly violate human rights in the interest of increased revenues. In many developing nations, the law enforcement and judicial apparatus necessary to ensure that transnational corporations comply with laws that protect individuals from harm is often weak or nonexistent. TNCs operating in such nations are often free to determine for themselves whether or not they will adhere to host nation laws designed to protect citizens from harm and guarantee their internationally recognized human rights. Direct and indirect human rights violations by TNCs are all too common. The office of the United Nations Special Representative of the Secretary-General on the issue of human rights and transnational corporations and other business enterprises examined 320 cases of alleged corporate human rights violations and found that TNCs "impact the full range of human rights ... including civil and political rights; economic, social and cultural rights; and labour rights" (Human Rights Council 2008: 2). Nearly 60% of these violations were directly caused by the firms through acts or omissions (Ibid., 4). The ability of TNCs to exploit governance gaps in this way has been a central concern of business ethics scholarship for many years.

In previous chapters, I synthesized existing business ethics scholarship regarding the human rights obligations of TNCs and other business enterprises and developed a series of arguments regarding business and human rights. I argued that TNCs have the ontological status necessary for moral agency and moral responsibility and that they are capable of either ignoring human rights obligations or of integrating human rights protections into their international operations. I argued that there are compelling reasons to believe that TNCs have agentically grounded moral obligations to respect basic human rights and also that there are sound social contract-based arguments for concluding that businesses have human rights obligations. The main conclusions of previous chapters are that TNCs are properly understood as corporate moral agents, capable of being duty bearers and entities morally responsible for their actions because they have internal decision structures, designed and managed by human agents, including the ethical infrastructure of the firm, corporate intentions understood primarily as plans, and the capacity for reflective assessment of corporate plans and practices. TNCs, in other words, are properly characterized as having human rights obligations, or duties, and should be held morally accountable for violating human rights, as well as praised and esteemed when their policies and practices protect human rights.

As noted above, Hsieh argues that we should "reject assigning human rights obligations to TNCs and their managers" (Hsieh 2015: 2019). Hsieh's core claim is that because only states can fully protect the equal standing of citizens (status egalitarianism), TNCs should not be regarded as having human rights obligations. I have argued that this claim is untenable because TNCs have direct human rights obligations to those with whom they interact, such as workers, customers, and those who live in the communities in which TNCs operate. This is a position shared by many scholars of business and human rights (Cragg 2004, 2009; Donaldson 1991; Santoro 2000; Wettstein 2009).

One of two things is true regarding Hsieh's account. Either Hsieh is stipulating that only states can have human rights obligations or he allows that entities other than states have human rights obligations. The former claim appears to be his position. He writes, "Status egalitarianism, however, is a claim against specific duty-bearers – namely, those with ability to enforce laws and those that have a responsibility to ensure the equal moral standing of individuals within their jurisdiction" (Hsieh 2017: 307). Since only states are perceived to have this legitimate authority, he surmises that only states have human rights obligations. However, there are good reasons for rejecting this position. To limit the class of actors with human rights obligations to states is to commit the fallacy of equivocation, since "human rights" are widely recognized in philosophical scholarship, in law, and in practical application, to have a meaning that allows them to be appropriately and legitimately applied to actors other than states. In business ethics scholarship, the attribution of human rights obligations to corporations was first made in a sustained manner by Donaldson over 30 years ago (Donaldson 1991). Peter Muchlinski (2001), along with other scholars, have pointed out that US law, for example, recognizes that corporations can directly violate human rights.

In Chapter Three, I pointed to the dangers of attributing to corporations the identical human rights obligations that states (or national governments) have, given the different functions of states and corporations in society. A failure to distinguish between the moral division of labor for human rights was a critical mistake of the United Nation's Working Group on the Methods and Activities of Transnational Corporations and its 2003 draft "Norms on the Responsibilities of Transnational Corporations and Other Business Enterprises with Regard to Human Rights" (2003). It was one of the features that lead to the demise of the "Draft Norms" and the creation of the mandate of the Special Representative of the Secretary-General on the issue of human rights and transnational corporations and other business enterprises.

To better understand the distinction between varieties of human rights obligations that exist, consider the different types of obligations that states themselves have. As Hsieh seems to acknowledge, not all states have the same human rights obligations. As he points out, states that meet their obligations and protect human rights have an obligation to intervene in states that fail to meet their human rights obligations (e.g. by engaging in or tolerating genocide). "In the case of states, the failure to uphold human rights provides grounds for intervention by other states despite claims of sovereignty" (Hsieh 2017: 304). States that routinely, or systematically, violate human rights do not have obligations to intervene in the same way, because they do not enjoy the same status as rights upholding states in the international order. Different varieties of states, then, have different human rights obligations. Why should it be supposed that if non-state actors have human rights obligations, they must be identical to those of state actors? The position of most business ethics scholars working in this area is that it is fallacious to claim that the obligations of corporations and states are identical, but it is equally fallacious to claim that TNCs and their managers have no human rights obligations.

This position is not a mere conceit or stipulation, it is based on the recognition that all international treaties regarding human rights are grounded in conceptions of human dignity that no person, group, or state may violate. For example, the Universal Declaration of Human Rights states that the basis for human rights is the "inherent dignity" and "equal and inalienable rights of all members of the human family" (United Nations General Assembly 1948). Article 30 states that "Nothing in this Declaration may be interpreted as implying for any State, group or person any right to engage in any activity or to perform any act aimed at the destruction of any of the rights and freedoms set forth herein" (Ibid.). In other words, even if one takes what Hsieh refers to as an "institutional approach" to human rights, persons, including managers, and groups, including corporations, have obligations not to violate human rights. However, they do not have the same obligations as states for the protection of the human rights of all citizens.

The language of international agreements among nations if often intentionally vague to allow for broad support, especially in the initial stages of policy development. The Brundtland definition of sustainability is a notorious example of a definition that allows for broad consensus, while at the same time remaining vague to the point of meaningless (Goodland 1995). For this reason, we should not be overly concerned that the "'Protect, Respect and Remedy'

Framework for Business and Human Rights" and its accompanying *Guiding Principles on Business and Human Rights* attributes "responsibilities" to corporations and "duties" to states (Human Rights Council 2011). As I argued in Chapter Three, the distinction between "responsibilities" and "duties" or obligations lacks a coherent conceptual basis, although it does serve to helpfully signal differences between corporate and state obligations. In light of the earlier failure of the Draft Norms, such signaling was likely necessary for an atheoretical document informed by pragmatism to achieve consensus in the United Nations Human Rights Council.

Hsieh claims that there may not be much disagreement between his position and the account of TNC human rights obligations that I have defended in previous chapters, in part, because he wants to distinguish between three different moral categories: "basic moral rights that ground duties on the part of TNCs," (Hsieh 2017: 308), human rights obligations, and human rights duties. For my part, it is important to rebut claims that TNCs have no human rights obligations and to point out that such a position is not theoretically justified. To be theoretically well motivated, at a minimum, sound, coherent, conceptual distinctions between *duties, obligations,* and *responsibilities* would need to be articulated and defended in light of existing human rights theory. The content and basis for distinguishing between these concepts, on Hsieh's account, remains obscure. As I have argued, the corporate "responsibility" to protect human rights articulated by the "Protect, Respect and Remedy" Framework is grounded merely in "social expectations" and in prudential risk management (Human Rights Council 2008). According to the tripartite framework, "Failure to meet this responsibility can subject companies to the courts of public opinion—comprising employees, communities, consumers, civil society, as well as investors—and occasionally to charges in actual courts" (Human Rights Council 2008: 16). The concept of corporate "responsibility" for human rights has no explicit moral or theoretical foundation in the "Protect, Respect and Remedy" Framework, so it seems odd and idiosyncratic to adapt the tripartite framework's pragmatic, politically motivated distinction in an effort to deny human rights obligations for TNCs.

Hsieh places special emphasis on jurisdiction, which following Samantha Besson, he defines as political and legal authority that claims to be or is perceived to be legitimate. Hsieh quotes Besson to explain that "jurisdiction consists in effective, overall and normative power or control (whether it is prescriptive, executive, or adjudicative). It amounts to more than the mere exercise of coercion or power, as a result: it also includes a normative dimension by reference to the imposition of reasons for action on its subjects and the corresponding appeal for compliance (Besson 2014: 254)." This normative dimension of jurisdiction is of special relevance for our analysis. What, we should ask, are the normatively legitimate reasons for holding TNCs accountable for human rights violations both domestically and across national borders in the host nations in which they operate?

One reasonable answer is that when TNCs fail to meet their human rights obligations to those individuals with whom they interact, they operate in a manner inconsistent with human dignity and are justly held accountable. That is, they fail to operate in a manner expected of all persons and groups and as such are appropriately held accountable by states because of this failure. This, after all, is the core justification of all internationally recognized human rights. To suggest otherwise would be to hold that there are *only* strategic reasons for TNCs to adhere to the rights articulated in the Universal Declaration of Human Rights, the International Covenant on Economic, Social and Cultural Rights, the International Covenant on Civil and Political Rights, and the International Labor Conventions. That is, it would be to hold that the only reasons TNCs and their managers have to adhere to the international system of human rights are that states and civil society will punish the TNCs and their managers in meaningful ways that outweigh firm profits and executive compensation. John Ruggie's approach in the "Protect, Respect and Remedy" Framework adapts this stance, a view that I criticized in Chapter 4.

Conclusion

The upshot of our analysis is that there are compelling arguments for attributing human rights obligations to TNCs and their managers that are not identical to the set of obligations that states have with respect to human rights and that it is logically difficult to deny this conclusion. At least, I have not seen a compelling argument against this conclusion. This is not to say that there are not important conceptual issues that remain to be addressed and which require our attention. The scope and limits of TNCs human rights obligations are important subjects and ones that merits further conceptual analysis and scholarly attention in a post-Westphalian international order, one in which the power and influence of TNCs continues to grow and in many instances challenges the power and influence of nation states. The next several chapters apply the cosmopolitan human rights framework to practical problems in international business.

Chapter Six

Labor Rights in Global Supply Chains

One of the most common and persistent ethical problems in international business concerns the working conditions and wages in the factories that are at the base of global supply chains, especially in consumer goods industries such as apparel, footwear, electronics, and toys. Commonly known as the "sweatshop problem," these contested matters include working conditions that are noncompliant with local labor laws, forced overtime, the suppression of collective bargaining rights, and wage theft. In the worst cases, workers are killed or injured by explosions, fires, malfunctioning machinery, and exposure to toxic substances, among other causes. The Rana Plaza disaster in Dhaka, Bangladesh, alone resulted in 1132 worker fatalities and injured more than 2500 workers. This chapter examines the ethics of health and safety, the disclosure of workplace hazards, the role of the rule of law in protecting workers, wage exploitation, and best practices in the management of labor rights in global supply chains.

Health and Safety

The modern sweatshop debate emerged at approximately the same time that economic globalization began to rapidly increase. One result of the outflow of capital from industrialized nations to developing nations was an increase in the number of textile mills and factories employing low-skilled workers to manufacture apparel, footwear, toys, electronics, and a variety of other consumer goods. These factories are sometimes owned by MNCs, but more often they are owned by entrepreneurs from newly industrialized nations, such as Taiwan and South Korea, or by indigenous entrepreneurs. In the 1990s, reports of abusive labor conditions in these factories emerged.

The Ethics of Global Business, First Edition. Denis G. Arnold.
© 2023 John Wiley & Sons Ltd. Published 2023 by John Wiley & Sons Ltd.

The Tae Kwang Vina Industrial, Ltd. shoe factory outside Ho Chi Min City in Vietnam is an illustrative example. This factory was built for the purpose of manufacturing Nike shoes under contract.[1] The factory employed 10 000 workers, most of them women, mainly between the ages of 18 and 24. Leaked documents from a Nike initiated audit of the factory found the following: Employment of underage workers, overtime work above the legally allowed maximum, underpayment of legal earnings, inadequate ventilation contributing to respiratory ailments, insufficient or absent safety equipment leading to exposure to airborne pollutants that cause neurological damage, toxic chemicals up to 177 times the legal standard, heat and noise well above legally maximums, missing fire extinguishers, and a lack of water for the use of workers (Ernst and Young 1997). Reports such as this, and others issued by nongovernmental organizations, led many consumers, shareholders, activists, NGOs, and labor experts to criticize multinational corporations and their contractors for the unethical treatment of workers in global supply chains. Critics allege that the basic dignity and human rights of workers are violated by such practices.[2]

In response to these criticisms, some economists and social theorists argue for a contrary conclusion.[3] They argue that the best way to enhance the overall welfare of the world's poorest populations is to increase the number of sweatshops in the developing world. The argument may be summarized as follows. All developing nations have a common, underexploited resource--large pools of unemployed or underemployed workers. To attract FDI, governments provide incentives such as export processing zones and free trade zones and negotiate international treaties that provide tariff relief. Most workers in factories producing goods for export were previously unemployed or making less money in the informal sector of local economies. Increased income for these workers results in increased spending that improves the local economy. As the local economy improves, the competition for workers increases. To secure the best workers, factories producing goods for export must improve working conditions. Poor and hazardous working conditions and low wages are, in this view, a necessary stage in the economic development of all nations. But it is also a temporary stage that will eventually be supplanted by improved working conditions and wages as economies grow.

This defense of the violation of basic rights in global supply chains is primarily an economic one and largely ignores the role that supply chain managers and TNC executives have on working conditions in supplier factories and the obligations they have to respect international labor rights. The duty of employers to provide safe working conditions is grounded in the basic right to physical security, the duty to provide a decent wage is ground in the basic right to subsistence, and the duty to permit workers to form unions and collectively bargain is grounded in the basic right to liberty. The "International Covenant on Economic, Social and Cultural Rights" provides clear, practical guidance regarding workers' rights including fair wages consistent with a "decent living" for workers and their families, "safe and healthy working conditions," "rest, leisure and reasonable limitation of working hours" (Article 7), and the right to collectively bargain and form trade unions (Article 8). Proponents of sweatshops ignore the legitimate, internationally recognized norm that employers must meet minimum deontic obligations to workers grounded in the basic rights of workers.

TNCs wield tremendous power over the owners and managers of such factories. Corporations normally dictate the quantity, quality, design, and delivery date of goods manufactured in overseas factories. This imbalance in power is partly due to an oversupply of export factories. The oversupply of factories is a result of a rapid increase in the number and size of export processing zones and free trade zones established by developing nations competing for jobs and foreign investment. Corporations can shop around for suppliers who charge the lowest prices for the specified quality goods delivered in the shortest amount of time after orders are placed. Factory owners are often locked in fierce competition for orders and frequently must accept the terms offered to them by large corporations or shut down in what is sometimes referred to as the "race to the bottom" in the global supply chain. While factory owners can provide low-cost safety features such as hazard signs and routine equipment maintenance, they may have difficulty providing costlier safety improvements (or adhering to local labor laws) if the financial terms dictated by the corporations are onerous. The coercive power that corporations exert has a causal relationship to the actual working conditions in contract factories. Given this causal relationship, it is reasonable to regard corporations as causally responsible for the safety standards of their contractors. If corporations are causally responsible for working conditions, and have the power to alter these conditions, they are morally responsible for the working conditions.

Intentionally or negligently subjecting workers to unsafe working conditions that are likely to result in injury or serious harm constitutes a *prima facie* violation of the duty not to injure or kill other persons. Workers have a dignity that machines and capital do not possess. When employers fail to protect workers adequately from workplace hazards, they treat workers more like objects with mere instrumental value, such as tools or raw materials, rather than as beings with intrinsic value and basic rights.[4] Respecting the dignity of workers entails at least two subordinate duties concerning safety and health. First, when workplace hazards exist, an employer has an obligation to inform workers in advance regarding workplace hazards so that individual workers can make informed decisions about the work and the conditions they find acceptable.[5] Second, employers have an obligation to ensure that basic health and safety conditions are met. Failing to do so violates the duty to refrain from harming workers.

Defenders of sweatshops assume that operating factories on a profit-maximizing basis always results in the enhanced welfare of workers. Such an *ex ante* assumption is unwarranted given the actual harm that can result to workers and surrounding communities. For example, workers at the Tae Kwang Vina factory were susceptible to long-term respiratory disease as a result of airborne fabric particles that were not properly vented and to permanent neurological damage resulting from direct exposure to excessive levels of toluene and other toxic chemicals. Workers at other factories routinely lose limbs by traumatic amputation, contract carpal tunnel syndrome from repetitive motion work, and experience hearing loss due to repeated exposure to noise pollution. In one case, an El Savadorean woman was refused medical attention when she miscarried at work. She brought the three-month-old fetus home at the end of her shift in clothing scraps where she and her family buried the fetus themselves.[6] When she and her colleagues sought to form a trade union, she was fired and the government destroyed their homes. The substantial and increasingly well-documented environmental harm caused to communities around some of these factories directly harms workers by polluting their ground water and indirectly by harming the environment in which their families live.[7] Defenders of sweatshops have yet to conduct *ex post* analyses of the aggregate impact of sweatshops on workers in specific labor markets, one that takes into account both the benefits and harms such employment brings to workers. Until such analyses are undertaken, the *ex ante* claims of sweatshop defenders should be regarded with skepticism. Furthermore, even if such studies were conducted and the *ex ante* predictions proved correct, this by itself would not demonstrate that the ethical obligations of employers have been met. For it is possible to enhance the welfare of impoverished persons without having discharged all of one's moral duties as an employer. For example, an employer may marginally improve the income of workers while simultaneously failing to disclose workplace hazards to the workers or physically punishing them for failing to meet production quotas.

Disclosing Workplace Hazards

Another perplexing feature of the arguments of most proponents of sweatshops is that they ignore the failure of employers to disclose hazards to workers. Workers at factories across the globe are routinely exposed to neurotoxins, carcinogens, dangerous or malfunctioning equipment, poor fire safety, or other hazards, without full disclosure of the risks of such work. Workers are routinely required to take hazardous jobs because of the adversity of their economic and social circumstances and lack of alternative employment opportunities. Theorists of widely divergent theoretical commitments agree that business owners have a moral obligation to disclose workplace hazards because a failure to disclose workplace hazards is a fraudulent representation of the terms of employment.[8] If one grants the fraudulent nature of such employment and the right of workers to be informed about workplace hazards prior to being employed, then such employment practices must be regarded as impermissible. However, defenders of sweatshops do not qualify their calls for more sweatshops with the stipulation that employers disclose workplace hazards to workers, nor do they provide reasons for thinking that the employers of sweatshop laborers should be exempted from this moral requirement.[9]

It remains to be determined which specific obligations employers owe workers with respect to the disclosure of workplace hazards. How much information ought to be shared with employees? The U.S. Department of Labor answers this question with a reasonable person standard.

> This standard is what a fair and informed member of the relevant community believes is needed. Under this standard, no employer, union, or other party should be held responsible for disclosing information beyond that needed to make an informed choice about the adequacy of safety precautions, industrial hygiene, long-term hazards, and the like, as determined by what the reasonable person in the community would judge to be the worker's need for information

(Faden and Beauchamp 2009: 129–136).

Such a standard has the obvious benefit of being suitable to a wide range of employees in a wide range of industries.

Ruth Faden and Tom Beauchamp defend a modified reasonable person standard.[10] They argue that the reasonable person standard fails to adequately deal with exposure to serious hazards where different workers may have different subjective needs. They argue that a reasonable person standard should be supplemented by a subjective standard whereby employees are invited to request any information pertinent to their individual circumstances. Employers have an obligation to provide employees with additional information based on the employees' individual circumstances and relevant needs.[11] These standards impose increasingly robust obligations on the employer. However, the use of a reasonable person standard for assessing the amount of information that should be communicated to workers is not without difficulty, even when modified to include the subjective standard recommended by Faden and Beauchamp. Questions arise when one attempts to establish what such a standard might amount to in different contexts. A reasonable person standard in the United States is likely to be very different from a reasonable person standard in nations with large populations of poorly educated or illiterate workers. For example, neurological damage from exposure to toxic chemicals is a risk for certain workers in shoe factories and electronics manufacturing, as well as many other types of industries. Workers unaware of these dangers will not know to ask for such information.

What sort of reasonable person standard could be applied in the global context? One solution is a Kantian standard grounded in the categorical imperative. On this approach one would determine which reasonable person standard is universalizable. The appropriate standard by which to measure universalizability in this instance is the pragmatic contradiction test.[12] A pragmatic contradiction occurs when one acts on principles that promote an action that is inconsistent with one's purpose when acted upon by all agents in similar circumstances. In other words, an employer or a country manager needs to ask themselves what information about occupational health and safety conditions they would want to be provided prior to deciding whether or not to accept a job. Call that baseline standard of information ß. If the employer or operations manager would not be willing to accept a world in which the amount of information disclosed to them on at least some occasions was <ß, then ß is the appropriate minimum standard of disclosure. This assumption is not unwarranted because employers or on-site mangers commonly understand better than others the actual working conditions and known hazards of a workplace. This account assumes that ß would be relatively constant across cultures since the risk to health and safety from the same toxic chemicals, injurious processes, or fires, is the same whether the worker is in Bangladesh, China, Mexico, El Salvador, or Ethiopia. Because of this asymmetry of information average employers, unlike average workers, are well situated to make a reasonable determination regarding appropriate workplace standards. This *universal disclosure standard*, then, constitutes an important ethical tool for corporations conducting global business.

Developing and newly industrialized nations often have large numbers of unemployed workers that will undertake almost any work in any conditions to better their circumstances. This raises an ethical problem that is not commonly encountered in developed nations where workers typically have more employment options and substantial social safety nets. The problem is this: even when appropriate disclosure takes place, workers will seldom enjoy the freedom to select better working conditions, even at lower wages, since the only alternative they have is destitution. In nations with significant governance gaps, corporations are often free to determine health and safety standards on their own or to utilize suppliers who put workers a jeopardy of injury and death because of poor working conditions. What occupational health and safety standards are corporations justified in utilizing in their global operations and supply chains?

If we grant that respecting the rights of workers, or treating them with dignity, requires that employers be concerned with the physical welfare of their employees, business owners have, at a minimum, a *prima facie* obligation to ensure that basic precautions are taken to protect the welfare of employees. To do otherwise would be to treat workers with callous disregard for their basic physical integrity. It might be objected that the fiduciary obligations to shareholders trump the obligation to improve working conditions for workers. However, if we keep in mind that these standards help prevent death and serious injuries, such as the loss of limbs and neurological damage from exposure to toxic chemicals, the *prima facie* duty of TNC managers to protect workers' rights consistent with the ILO Conventions and the International Bill of Human Rights.

The Rule of Law

Defenders of sweatshops either deny or tacitly approve the widespread violation of local labor laws that take place in global sweatshops, such as at the Tae Kwan Vina factory.[13] The widespread violations of local labor laws regarding wages and benefits, working hours, collective bargaining, and worker safety have been well documented.[14] When Gap began to assess and report on vendor compliance with local labor laws, it found that between 25 and 50% of its contract factories lacked full compliance with local labor laws in North Asia; Southeast Asia; the Indian Sub-Continent; Sub-Saharan Africa; Mexico, Central America, and the Caribbean; and South America. In China, more than 50% of its contract factories lacked full compliance with local labor laws.[15] These violations were taking place in a context in which Gap was attempting to ensure full compliance with local labor laws. If a company expends considerable resources to ensure that local labor laws are followed and fails to garner greater compliance than Gap has thus far achieved, it is reasonable to surmise that violations are more widespread in factories working for multinationals that are not seeking to ensure compliance with local labor laws.

The tacit approval of labor law violations is a perplexing feature of pro-sweatshop arguments because it is difficult to justify widespread violations of the law. For example, Milton Friedman, the iconic defender of a libertarian view of business ethics in which the primary obligation of corporations is to maximize profits in the interest of shareholders, denies that it is legitimate for corporations to violate the law.[16] Friedman's position is grounded in the idea that citizens and responsive democracies determine the laws that should govern corporate behavior. Indeed, this is a seldom referenced or discussed element of the justification of the shareholder primacy view. Corporations, in this view, have no legitimate basis for undermining or contravening the will of the people by violating democratically determined laws.

When a firm contract with factories in developing nations, there is a presumption that they do so with an understanding of the legal framework in place and the expectation that their own legal rights will be enforced and protected. As a matter of consistency, companies have a *prima facie* obligation to respect the legal framework they themselves call upon for protection (e.g. property rights and contract rights).[17] There are, of course, unjust laws where people of good conscience can agree that the most ethical course of action is to ignore the law. However, this is not the case with respect to laws governing the compensation and safety of workers in developing nations. These laws are intended to provide workers with minimum working conditions and wages to ensure, in the words of the International Labour Organization, "decent and productive work, in conditions of freedom, equity, security and human dignity" (International Labour Organization 1999). These laws are central to the international human rights regime that helps protect human dignity at the global level.

Improving Working Conditions

Many companies that have either outsourced or moved the production of labor-intensive goods, such as apparel, footwear, and furniture, from the United States and Europe to Asia and Latin America have considerable expertise in occupational safety. This expertise can be utilized to improve working conditions in factories operating in nations with little occupational safety expertise. Companies such as Nike, adidas, Pentland, and Gap have publicly committed to utilizing their expertise in overseas factories. These companies have implemented low-cost safety improvements, and some claim to have raised the standards in overseas factories to meet or exceed US OSHA standards. For example, in 1998 Nike, partly in response to criticism that resulted from its leaked Tae Kwan Vina factory audit, promised to adapt the personal exposure limits of OSHA as the standard for indoor air quality at all footwear factories.[18] Nike has clearly improved the working conditions in many of its factories.[19] In 2019, Nike was implementing programs to allow workers to share in productivity gains. None of these companies has identified cost as a barrier to enhancing workplace safety. The main implementation barrier that is identified by companies is directly related to the lax safety standards that were previously tolerated. For example, when Gap first began to release public reports about its efforts to ensure compliance in all of its factories with its "Code of Vendor Conduct," it found that it was difficult to garner vendor compliance with its own code and with local labor laws.[20] Contract factories that had long operated without strict enforcement of occupational safety rules and procedures found it difficult to embrace a culture of enhanced safety.

The efforts undertaken by Nike, Gap, and other companies to improve working conditions in factories that they did not own but instead contracted with to manufacture their products raise important questions about moral responsibility. In particular, is it reasonable to hold such companies accountable for their contractors' treatment of workers? It has been argued that given that the corporation has done something positive for the workers by providing them with jobs, it is unreasonable to expect anything more from the corporation in the way of fair treatment of contract factory workers in developing nations.[21] According to proponents of this view, "It is unreasonable to expect any bargain struck between two parties to redress every issue of fairness or desert that may apply to one party. [Corporations] are in some sense "taking advantage" of background conditions in the Third World when they outsource their production, but this alone does not make them responsible for the poverty that makes their sourcing decisions profitable."[22] In other words, if the unsafe working conditions are a standard feature of work in these nations, the corporations that outsource to these factories, and take advantage of these lower standards, ought not to be burdened with additional obligations that are the responsibility of governments. This argument implies that if the terms of the contract preclude the possibility that the contract factory can provide, the legally mandated wages, working hours, and working conditions, the illegal labor practices would not be the responsibility of the corporation. In fact, the last 15 years have seen a major transformation in the management of the health and safety labor practices of many multinational corporations. Companies such as Nike, adidas, Gap, and Mattel have publicly committed to respecting local labor laws, improving working conditions, monitoring factories, and reporting on their efforts in annual social reports.[23] They join companies such as LeviStrauss and Motorola, which have always sought to ensure the health and safety of workers in their supply chains.

One of the most comprehensive and successful reorganizations of health and safety systems by any corporation in recent years has taken place at Mattel. The company created Global Manufacturing Principles for its production facilities and contract manufacturers. It then spent millions of dollars to upgrade its manufacturing facilities to improve worker health, safety, and comfort. It also facilitated the creation of a comprehensive independent external monitoring program to help ensure that it would meet its self-imposed standards.[24] Mattel has empowered the safety auditors of its factories and suppliers to publish all of their findings without regard to content. In this way, Mattel has made its efforts to improve working conditions transparent. The examples of such companies are, perhaps, the best responses to those social theorists who cling to the idea that economic growth in developing nations must inevitably come at the cost of the safety and welfare of workers.

In summary, the main arguments that defenders of sweatshops deploy are unpersuasive. Further, defenders of sweatshops tend to make unwarranted assumptions that, once understood and analyzed, further undermine their claims. The exercise of corporate power in developing nations plays a large role in determining the working conditions in overseas factories. Corporations that fail to exercise that power in such a way as to help ensure that factory conditions are compatible with the basic rights or dignity of workers are properly regarded as blameworthy for their actions. Further, the claims of sweatshop defenders are undermined by the many corporations, in a variety of industries, that routinely expend substantial corporate resources to help ensure safe and healthy working conditions for workers. Evidence demonstrates that corporations can help protect the welfare of workers in their global supply chain while remaining economically competitive. But what about wages? Do corporations have obligations to ensure that these workers are paid an ethically appropriate wage? If so, can they afford to pay such wages while remaining economically competitive? These questions will be taken up in the last major section of this chapter.

Exploitative Wages

One of the most contentious issues concerning global sweatshops is the question of whether workers are paid exploitative wages. Historically, the concept of exploitation has often been connected to the work of Karl Marx. His account of exploitation holds that capitalists exploit workers by expropriating the bulk of worker productivity, or what Marx referred to as their surplus labor. In this view, regular technological innovation results in labor-saving manufacturing techniques that ensure large pools of unemployed workers. The unemployed are forced to choose between accepting subsistence wages or remaining unemployed. Capitalists benefit from the surplus labor of workers, and workers have little choice but to accept meager wages. There is controversy among Marx's interpreters as to whether or not Marx thought exploitation was unjust, though it seems clear that he believed that exploitation undermines human flourishing.[25] Critics of Marxian accounts of exploitation argue that such accounts ignore the risks involved in capital investment and fail to acknowledge the importance of managerial expertise for profitable business enterprises.

In recent years, the debate over the nature and moral significance of exploitation has shifted away from Marxian accounts. The most influential non-Marxian account of exploitation is provided by Alan Wertheimer.[26] Wertheimer restricts his account to mutually advantageous exchanges typical of market transactions. In such transactions, both parties gain something from the transaction, even if one party gains considerably more than the other party. Wertheimer argues that exploitation takes place when one person takes *unfair* advantage of another person relative to a specific baseline or standard. Because fairness is a moral consideration, Wertheimer's theory of exploitation is moralized.[27] The moral baseline that Wertheimer defends is that of a hypothetical market price that would be generated by an imperfect competitive market, one in which buyers and sellers lack perfect information.[28] This hypothetical market price is intended to reflect the cost of providing a service, as well as the price informed consumers are willing to pay in reasonably competitive circumstances. Such a price is to be differentiated from the price generated in a perfectly competitive market, a market in which the many buyers and sellers have perfect information.[29] This baseline is not intended to reflect a principle of desert or justice. Instead, this baseline "is a price at which neither party takes special unfair advantage of particular defects in the other party's decision-making capacity or special vulnerabilities in the other party's situation."[30] Exploitation, on this account, always involves taking special unfair advantage of at least one party in a mutually advantageous market transaction. An example will help to illustrate this view. Imagine a tow-truck driver who comes across a stranded motorist in a snowstorm. The stranded motorist has no means to call for help. The tow-truck driver offers to tow the motorist to safety for ten times the prevailing towing fee in that area. The driver, facing dire circumstances, accepts the offer. On Wertheimer's account, this transaction is exploitative because the driver took special unfair advantage of the stranded motorist, charging that individual a rate well in excess of the hypothetical market price. And since exploitation is always morally objectionable on a moralized view, the driver is morally blameworthy.

Are sweatshop workers paid exploitative wages on Wertheimer's account? To focus our discussion, consider the well-known cases of alleged exploitation of sweatshop workers by Nike in Indonesia. Critics alleged that a Nike contractor paid employees the equivalent of $2.60 per day in Jakarta, Indonesia, while the amount necessary to cover basic food, clothing, and shelter needs at that time was approximately $4.00 per day.[31] Assume, for the sake of argument, that these facts are correct. On Wertheimer's account, Nike contract workers in Jakarta were not exploited because they benefit from their employment and the wages they earn are generated by a competitive labor market.[32] The workers freely choose to work for Nike's contractors in Indonesia because the wages they earn are better than those they could make elsewhere. One implication of understanding exploitation in this way is that it is not possible to pay a worker exploitative wages if workers voluntarily show up for work in a minimally competitive labor market. In other words, Wertheimer's position is just the opposite of Marx's: Capitalists never exploit workers, at least with respect to wages in minimally competitive labor markets.

One might object to this conclusion by pointing out that during the period in question, Indonesia had an authoritarian government that suppressed dissent with the aid of the military. Human rights violations were widespread and government policies created significant barriers to union organizing.[33] Given these unjust background conditions and a lack of negotiating power, one might argue that the workers were forced to accept the Nike contractor's terms. A critic also might argue that Nike exploited the workers by taking advantage of their desperate circumstances. Wertheimer's response is that unjust or unfair background conditions do not necessarily result in exploitative agreements. On his account, unless Nike and its contractors take special unfair advantage of the Indonesian workers, their agreement should be regarded as fair.[34] Some readers may find an account of exploitation that reaches these conclusions regarding Nike's Indonesian workers implausible and unworthy of consideration. Nonetheless, Wertheimer's account of exploitation has been utilized to argue that few, if any, sweatshop workers are exploited.[35] Furthermore, Wertheimer's position tends to support the presumption of libertarians who believe that so long as workers are not physically forced to enter the factory each day their wages cannot be regarded as exploitative.[36]

On Wertheimer's theory of exploitation, if one party exploits another the exploiter is morally blameworthy in all cases. However, the idea of justified exploitation is consistent with ordinary language use of the term. For example, we do not normally criticize a chess player who exploits a defect in the strategy of an opponent (within the rules of the game) of acting unfairly. This feature of our understanding of the concept of exploitation is part of the reason that many theorists defend a non-moralized view. In contrast to moralized theories, empirical theories do not settle the question of the moral status of the act. Empirical theories of social concepts maintain that the criteria for determining whether a particular phenomenon has occurred rest in an evaluation of the facts involved and do not depend upon moral baseline or standards.

Perhaps the most compelling empirical account of exploitation has been defended by Allen Wood. According to Wood, exploitation occurs when one person takes advantage of the weakness or vulnerability of another to derive some benefit from the target of exploitation.[37] In this case, the question of whether exploitation takes place depends upon factual matters, such as the individual's level of vulnerability measured in categories such as economic or social power. Wood's empirical theory of exploitation suggests a different conclusion regarding the case of Nike's workers in Indonesia. On his account, Nike exploited the workers in their Indonesian factories because it took advantage of the workers impoverished circumstances to benefit from their cheap labor. According to Wood, "Marx was right: Capital virtually always exploits wage labor. At least this is self-evident if it is granted that those who own the means of production enjoy a decisive bargaining advantage over those who own little besides their capacity to labor, and that this fundamental vulnerability on the part of labor decisively influences the terms of wage contracts."[38]

According to Wood, exploitation is morally objectionable when it is disrespectful of others.[39] Popular criticism of the wages paid to sweatshop workers is frequently grounded in a belief that these workers are treated disrespectfully, like disposable tools of production. As we saw above, Kant and his interpreters have provided a philosophical defense of the idea that the basic dignity of persons should be respected. Anyone concerned with the dignity of workers needs to determine what compensation would be consistent with respectful treatment. How many hours should employees be required to work each week? What minimum wage should they be paid for a work week? Elsewhere I have argued that to respect workers, employers must provide wages that enable them to meet basic needs and satisfy certain capabilities necessary for their well-being. Specifically, Norman Bowie and I have argued, that at a minimum, respecting employees requires that they be paid wages for a 48-hour work week that allows two working adults to keep an average sized family out of overall poverty.[40] Thus, two parents would earn sufficient income to ensure that their average sized family can afford basic food needs, shelter, clothing, energy, transportation, and basic health care with an additional 10% for discretionary spending.[41] Having these needs met helps to ensure the physical well-being and independence of employees, contributes to the development of their rational capacities, and provides them with the necessary conditions for the cultivation of self-esteem. So, while it may be true that multinational corporations exploit the labor pools of developing nations in order to gain competitive advantages, and consumers reward such companies by purchasing lower priced goods, companies that pay wages compatible with human dignity, while ensuring decent working conditions, do nothing wrong.

Defenders of sweatshops commonly assume that higher wages will result in increased unemployment. Given these assumptions, it is important to consider relevant economic considerations. While it is not possible to canvas the range of economic issues relevant to this debate, it will be helpful to briefly address some pertinent issues. The labor cost of production for a sweatshirt that retails for $35.00 has been put at .45¢, or 1.29% of the retail value.[42] Because the increase in labor costs necessary to ensure that workers are paid a living wage is comparatively small as a percentage of retail value, workers' rights advocates argue that the cost of providing a living wage is sufficiently small as to be absorbed as an operating expense. Productivity gains can offset such a modest increase in costs. "Put simply, workers whose minimum daily dietary require-ments are met and who have basic non-food needs met, will have more energy and better attitudes at work; will be less likely to come to work ill; and will be absent with less frequency."[43] Defenders of sweatshops respond by arguing that no matter how small the costs, voluntary increases in wages must result in lower employment by firms as they seek to offset increased costs.[44]

Such views tend to presuppose that corporations always operate with instru-mental practical reason, but as was argued above such a view is not plausible. Many corporations explicitly recognize ethical constraints regarding their treatment of employees and did so prior to being publicly criticized for disre-spectful labor practices. It is also the case that defenders of sweatshops tend to ground their arguments in textbook economics, rather than in actual studies of labor markets. Few studies have been conducted of labor markets in which corporations have voluntarily increased wages. However, one recent study found that when wages were voluntarily increased in Indonesian contract factories as a result of anti-sweatshop campaigns, employment levels actually increased as a result.[45] In cases in which such increased costs cannot be easily absorbed as operating expenses and in which increased productivity does not offset the increase in labor costs, evidence demonstrates that the costs may be passed on to consumers via higher retail prices.[46]

Conclusion

If we grant that workers enjoy basic rights such as freedom, noninjury, and well-being, then employers have a duty to ensure that minimum health and safety conditions are maintained in the workplace. Given that many workers are forced to take hazardous work, and given that some companies in capital intensive industries may not be able to stay in business if they voluntarily improve health and safety conditions, OSHA-type standards are typically justified in industrialized nations. In many developing nations, OSHA-type standards cannot reasonably be enforced by local governments. In such contexts, corporate employers have a duty to help ensure that respectful health and safety conditions are in place in their global supply chains. Further, all employees are entitled to be informed in the hiring process of the workplace hazards they will encounter in manner consistent with the universal disclosure standard. Finally, the respectful treatment of workers requires that they be paid a weekly wage consistent with basic human dignity. Such a wage may or may not exceed the minimum wage in developing nations, but when it does exceed the minimum wage there are good reasons for believing that corporations have a duty to ensure that the appropriate above minimum wage is paid to these workers. Companies that fulfill these minimal duties will play a constructive role in reducing the millions of workplace injuries and deaths that occur across the globe each year, as well as the exploitation to which countless others are subjected.

Notes

1. Nike helped pioneer the concept of a consumer goods company that emphasizes design and marketing, but does not itself manufacture any of the products that it sells.
2. Human Rights Watch 1998; Conner 2002; National Labor Committee 1995. See, For example Santoro 2000; Arnold 2003 a, b; Arnold and Bowie 2003; Arnold and Hartman 2003; Sethi 2003; Arnold and Hartman 2005; Arnold and Hartman 2006.

3. See, For example Maitland 2009; Krugman 1999; Kristof 2000; Academic Consortium on International Trade 2000; Henderson 2001; Norberg 2003; Bhagwati 2004.
4. For discussion see Raz 2001. For an account of respect that owes much to Kant, but is intended to be pluralistic in the sense that it is compatible with a wide range of ethical theories, see Ruth Sample, *Exploitation: What It is and Why It's Wrong*, 2003.
5. Machan 1987. Libertarian business ethicists, such as Machan, typically appeal to the work of Nozick in defending negative rights. Nozick famously defends the view that all persons have negative rights, but that positive rights come into existence only when people voluntarily agree to undertake the obligations that correspond to such rights (e.g., through valid contracts). What is much less well understood is that, to the extent that he grounds such rights, Nozick does so by utilizing Kant's doctrine of respect for persons: "Side constraints upon action reflect the underlying Kantian principle that individuals are ends and not merely means; they may not be sacrificed or used for the achieving of others ends without their consent. Individuals are inviolable." See Nozick et al. 1974: 30–31; see also Cohen 1987.
6. Juan Salvat, Peter Breuls, and Soeteway. *Free Trade Slaves*. 1988.
7. There are negative externalities for others members of local populations as well. See, for example Spencer, 2007.
8. Anderson 1995; Cohen 1987; Machan 1987.
9. See, e.g., Maitland 1997; Krugman 1999; Kristof 2000; Henderson 2001; Norberg 2003; Bhagwati 2004.
10. Faden and Beauchamp 2009.
11. Faden and Beauchamp 2009: 132.
12. Herman 1993: 47.
13. Bhagwati (2004: 173) explicitly denies that such violations take place. Nearly, all other defenders of sweatshops cited in this chapter ignore the issue.
14. For discussion see Arnold and Hartman 2006: 686–90.
15. In 2003, between 25 and 50% of its contract factories lacked full compliance with local labor laws in North Asia; Southeast Asia; the Indian Sub-Continent; Sub-Saharan Africa; Mexico, Central America and the Caribbean; and South America. In China, more than 50% of its contract factories lacked full compliance with local labor laws. Gap Inc., (Social Responsibility Report 2003).
16. Friedman 1970.
17. For a defense of this view, see Arnold and Bowie 2003: 227–228.
18. Philip Knight 1998.
19. See Laura P. Hartman and Richard E. Wokutch, "Nike, Inc.: Corporate Social Responsibility and Workplace Standard Initiatives in Vietnam," In Hartman, et al., *Rising Above Sweatshops* (2003) pp. 145–90. See also, *Purpose Moves Us: Nike, Inc. FY 2019 Impact Report* (2020).
20. In 2003, between 25 and 50% of its contract factories lacked full compliance with local labor laws in North Asia; Southeast Asia; the Indian Sub-Continent; Sub-Saharan Africa; Mexico, Central America and the Caribbean; and South America. In China, more than 50% of its contract factories lacked full compliance with local labor laws. Gap Inc. *Social Responsibility Report* 2003.
21. Sollar's and Englander 2007: 9.

22. Sollar's and Englander 2007: 9.
23. For case studies highlighting positive, proactive labor practices at companies such as Nike, Levis Strauss, adidas, Dow Chemical, and Chiquita, see Hartman, Arnold, and Wokutch, eds, 2003.
24. Sethi 1999: 225–241; Sethi 2003.
25. Arneson 1981: 202–27; Roemer 1982; Schwartz 1995: 275–307; Nelson and Ware 1997.
26. Wertheimer 1996. For an alternative moralized account of exploitation see Sample, *Exploitation*. Sample characterizes exploitation as disrespectful interaction. Her account is an improvement over Wertheimer's insofar as it is able to account for exploitative relationships and not merely exploitative transactions. However, her view has the same defect as all moralized account of exploitation insofar as it cannot account for morally neutral cases of exploitation. Furthermore, if exploitation always involves disrespect, little seems to be added to the concept of disrespect by calling it exploitative.
27. Wertheimer defends a moralized theory of coercion in *Coercion*. For an outline of an empirical theory of coercion, see Arnold, "Coercion and Moral Responsibility."
28. Wertheimer 1996: 230.
29. Wertheimer 1996: 217. A hypothetical market price "abstracts from some features of an actual market, such as defects in information and non competitiveness, [but] it does not abstract from other background characteristics of the buyers and sellers, such as risk." Wertheimer, 1996: 231.
30. Wertheimer 1996: 230.
31. Varley 1998: 258-59.
32. Defenders of sweatshops such as Matt Zwolinski and Benjamin Powell assume that such labor markets are competitive, but it is not clear that such an assumption is warranted. In many nations, employers have monopsony power over workers. For discussion of the concept of monopsony power in labor markets (Boal and Ransom 1997: 86–122; Zwolinski 2007: 689–727; Powell 2006: 215–221.
33. Varley 1998: 215–221.
34. Wertheimer 1996: 298–299)].
35. Zwolinski 2007.
36. Zwolinski 2007; Maitland 1997.
37. Wood 2004, 141–47.
38. Wood 2004, 155.
39. Wood 2004, 151.
40. Arnold and Bowie 2003: 233–239; Arnold and Bowie, Arnold and Bowie 2007; See also Arnold and Hartman 2006.
41. This does not entail that both parents would be working in a factory. For example, one person might remain at home carrying for young children while working a field or tending to a cottage industry. It is likely that any living wage standard would need to be attentive to the options available to the spouses and factory workers in different areas and regions in order to meet the goals of the wage. The general topic of an area or context specific living wages is one that deserves considerably more attention from scholars that it has received.

42. Rolph 2007.
43. Arnold and Bowie 2003: 237. For more detailed discussion and additional sources see this article.
44. Powell "Sweatshop Sophistries" and Sollars and Englander, "Sweatshops."
45. Harrison and Scorse 2006: 158.
46. One study of this issue found that consumers are willing to pay increased prices for products made under good working conditions. See Pollin et al. 2004: 153–71.

Chapter Seven

Corporate Social Responsibility at the Base of the Pyramid

The base of the pyramid (BoP) proposition (Prahalad and Hart 2002; Prahalad and Hammond 2002) holds that transnational companies (TNCs) can exploit neglected entrepreneurial opportunities while simultaneously alleviating poverty by serving billions of previously ignored customers living in poverty. Prahalad (2004) describes the BoP as an invisible market of four billion people living on less than $2 per day, waiting to be tapped. London and Hart (2004) describe it as a huge base of potential customers earning less than $1500 PPP (purchasing power parity) per year. BoP strategies are recommended as win–win market opportunities that allow TNCs to do well by doing good. It is claimed that pursuing BoP strategies "means lifting billions of people out of poverty and desperation" (Prahalad and Hart 2002) and enhancing the "dignity and choice" of the poor via access to more goods and services (Prahalad 2004). At the core of the BoP proposition is the idea that socially responsible TNCs can simultaneously improve their profitability while benefitting the global poor. But, as will be argued, the validity of this claim depends on the specific BoP business venture, the ethical framework that is utilized to analyze the venture, and the theory of corporate social responsibility that is employed.

Given a lack of uniformity in the literature regarding the size and the purchasing power of the BoP, this chapter begins by clarifying the scope of the BoP and the poorest segments of consumers within the BoP: those living in moderate and extreme poverty as defined by the World Bank. Next, research in development economics and consumer behavior is utilized to characterize the vulnerability of the moderately and extremely poor (MEP). Karnani (2007) has claimed that the poor may be wrongly exploited by TNCs targeting the BoP, but the theoretical basis for claiming that some products or services are exploitative, while others are not, is unclear from his analysis. This chapter

The Ethics of Global Business, First Edition. Denis G. Arnold.
© 2023 John Wiley & Sons Ltd. Published 2023 by John Wiley & Sons Ltd.

provides an account of exploitation that explains why marketing some products or services to the MEP is properly regarded as wrongfully exploitative. An exploitative approach is contrasted with an empowerment approach that respects the human rights of the MEP. A capabilities analysis is utilized to develop empowerment strategies for BoP ventures consistent with respect for human rights. A theory of serving the MEP grounded in the empowerment of the poor is defended and a multi-stage opportunity assessment process for implementing morally legitimate BoP ventures is developed. Finally, an empowerment theory of BOP ventures targeting the MEP developed in this chapter is utilized to demonstrate the inadequacy of the instrumental, or economic, conception of corporate social responsibility (CSR) and to defend an ethical conception of CSR.

Poverty and Vulnerability at the Base of the Pyramid

The extremely poor live on less than $1.25 per day, the moderately poor survive on less than $2.00 per day, and together they constitute a market of 2.6 billion people (The World Bank 2011). The limited purchasing power of the extremely poor has led some researchers to conclude that BoP strategies are unlikely to be helpful to them (Santos and Laczniak 2009). More commonly, researchers implicitly or explicitly presume that the moderately and extremely poor, as well as those earning slightly more than $2.00 per day, will benefit from having a wider range of consumer choices made available to them. However, the concept of "benefit" is ill-defined in the literature and the assumption that products or services purchased by the poor are beneficial to them is widespread (Prahalad 2004; Ireland 2008). The implication seems to be that the MEP are much like Western middle-class consumers, only with fewer consumer choices and less purchasing power. This characterization of people living in extreme poverty is unwarranted. Considerable research has been undertaken on the social and economic experiences of people surviving on incomes below $1.25 or $2.00 per day (Banerjee and Duflo 2007, 2011; Collins et al. 2009; Narayan et al. 2000). This research provides valuable insights into the spending habits, mindsets, and vulnerabilities of the MEP and provides much needed context for assessing the ethical dimensions of targeting the poor as consumers.

The Size and Nature of the BoP Market

There is a lack of consensus in the BoP literature regarding the size and income levels of the market. This lack of clarity can lead to inconsistency in the analysis of business ventures directed at the BoP. Researchers often introduce their work with different statistics on the population, spending power, and income levels of those at the BoP. For example, Prahalad and Hart (2002) define the BoP as 4 billion people living on less than $1500 per year and this figure is used by Anderson and Markides (2006), London and Hart (2004), and Seelos and Mair (2007). Prahalad (2004) defines the BoP as 4 billion people living on less than $2.00 per day and this figure is used by Altman et al. (2009), Stefanovic et al. (2007), Webb et al. (2009).

Hammond et al. (2007) define the BoP as 4 billion people living on less than $3000 per year and this figure is used by Fitch and Sorensen (2007). Some of the variation in the literature can be attributed to the base year for purchasing power parity (PPP), but this does not explain the large deviation from World Bank data commonly cited in the development economics and poverty literature. The World Bank has published the so-called dollar per day and two dollar per day poverty lines since 1981. Estimates from 2002 showed 2.8 billion people living on less than $2.00 per day, not four billion (The World Bank 2011). The current World Bank population estimate for those living below $2.00 per day is 2.6 billion (The World Bank 2011).

Clarity regarding the size and purchasing power of the BoP is helpful for at least two reasons. First, clarity provides a reliable basis for assessing the size of the market opportunity and evaluating the feasibility of the BoP proposition for TNCs. Prahalad (2004) estimates BoP spending power to be $13 trillion. Our analysis of World Bank data showed that those living below $2.00 per day totaled 2.8 billion at that time. Thus, we conclude that the size of the market opportunity for TNCs is overstated using Prahalad's estimate of a BoP population of 4 billion living below $2.00 per day.

Hammond et al. (2007) estimate BoP spending power to be $5 trillion based on a population of 4 billion people living below $9.05 per day and Karnani (2007) defines the BoP in 2005 as 2.6 billion people living below $2.00 per day along with the World Bank and estimates their spending power to be $1.42 trillion in PPP terms (The World Bank 2011). Because Karnani (2007) estimates are derived using the same PPP base year as Hammond et al. (2007), those living between $2.00 per day and $9.05 per day would represent $3.58 trillion in spending power at PPP terms. If the BoP is taken to include this segment as well, it is a much larger market opportunity. However, the issue is not merely defining the scope of the BoP but differentiating between market segments in order to better understand the needs of individuals living at different levels of poverty (Kotler et al. 2006). The differences in the needs and purchasing power of, for example, individuals living at $6.00 per day versus those living at $1.25 per day are significant and should inform entrepreneurial TNCs seeking to serve these markets.

A second reason for clarifying the size and purchasing power of the BoP is to facilitate the assessment of the ethics of TNCs exploiting market opportunities among populations living at different levels of deprivation. Targeting vulnerable groups raises distinctive ethical issues. As with any vulnerable consumer group, such as children, the elderly, or the handicapped, BoP populations are particularly susceptible to harm to their well-being from market transactions relative to less vulnerable populations. Their vulnerability may be exacerbated if they are also very young, old, or handicapped. In his extended theoretical analysis of the concept, Brenkert defines the vulnerable in market exchanges as those with "qualitatively different experiences, conditions, and/or incapabilities, which impede their abilities to participate in normal adult market activities" (Brenkert 1998: 13). The vulnerable are less able to protect their own interests and are susceptible to being "swayed, moved or enticed in directions which might benefit others but which might harm their interests" (p. 14) as a result of their unique circumstances. Individuals at the BoP are both cognitively and socially vulnerable.

The cognitive vulnerability of those living at the BoP is a feature of illiteracy or limited education. The illiteracy rate in nations with high BoP populations is substantial. In Bangladesh that rate is 52%, for India 39%, and for Nigeria 32% for those 15 and older (CIA 2011). Poverty makes it difficult to attain education, even when it is provided at no cost by governments, because of the need of children to leave school to help support families (where the median size is between seven and eight), because of poor quality education, and because of the inability of illiterate or partially literate parents to support their children's education (Banerjee and Duflo 2007). Educational opportunities are also lost when young children are bartered, sold, or orphaned, as a result of the desperate poverty of their parents.

Social vulnerability is a result of poverty itself. Poor consumers spend to compensate for their penury and to feel a sense of belonging. Chakravarti (2006), drawing from Sen (1999) argues, "the psychological reality of the BoP is revealed in sub-normative choices, self-defeating preference structures, and confused contradictions and preference reversals that block paths to self-improvement" (p. 367). In a study of Brazilians living on less than US$8 per day, Barki and Parente (2010) found that the poor have "a stronger need to compensate for a dignity deficit and low self-esteem" and "a high level of aspiration to feel socially included in society" (p. 21). These psychological traits make them vulnerable to market transactions that can undermine their well-being by reducing their ability to consume basic goods.

The Composition of the BoP and the MEP

To better assess ethical issues that arise in serving BoP consumers, providing an account of the composition of the BoP is necessary. In order to resolve the inconsistencies discussed above, and to provide clarity with respect to the analysis undertaken in this chapter, the BoP is defined in the following terms. Consistent with Hammond et al., the entire BoP is defined as the population of 4 billion people earning less than $9.05 per day ($3260 per year at 2005 PPP) who primarily transact in the informal market economy.

However, rather than use the problematic segmentation of the BoP by Hammond et al., our analysis is grounded in the economics and poverty literature that already enjoys broad academic support. Consistent with standard usage in development economics, moderate poverty is defined as those earning $1.25 to $2.00 per day and extreme poverty as those earning less than $1.25 per day (Figure 7.1). This allows for the clear identification of the most vulnerable members of the BoP: those living in moderate or extreme poverty (MEP). Approximately 1.4 billion people live in extreme poverty and 1.2 billion people living moderate poverty for a global population of 2.6 billion MEP.

Our representation of the BoP differs from *The Next 4 Billion* (Hammond et al. 2007) by utilizing fewer segments. Hammond et al. use six annual income segments to describe the BoP: $500, $1000, $1500, $2000, $2500, and $3000. While we find that these income segments are beneficial, only 36 countries have population and expenditure data for each segment. For the many countries for which population and expenditure data are not provided, researchers can only deduce the population figures for the entire BoP ($3000 and below) without knowing what percentage of the population belongs to each income segment completely. In our alternative approach, we utilize World Bank data to establish tiers 4 and 5, which describe the MEP within the BoP. This approach uses household survey data from 115 countries and thereby represents a more robust picture of the MEP than the 36 countries used in Hammond et al. 2007.

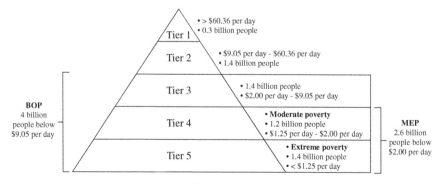

Figure 7.1   The Economic Pyramid.

Vulnerabilities of the Moderately and Extremely Poor

Research by poverty and development scholars shows that the MEP live in a cycle of poverty and deprivation that causes cognitive and social vulnerability. Adults and children living in moderate and extreme poverty are subjected to a state of mental distress, depression, and a feeling of hopelessness, which ultimately affects well-being and alters their ability to aspire to a better life (Narayan et al. 2000). For the most part, the MEP are excluded from the formal market economy; instead, operating in a web of informal networks. "They have houses but not titles; crops but not deeds; businesses but not statutes of incorporation" (de Soto 2000: 7). Often times, the MEP are socially excluded and taken advantage of by other poor members in the society who are marginally better off. According to Sachs (2005: 20), "They cannot meet their basic needs for survival. They are chronically hungry; unable to access health care, lack the amenities of safe drinking water and sanitation, cannot afford education for some or all of the children, and perhaps lack rudimentary shelter."

The harm to well-being, to which the MEP are susceptible because of their vulnerability, may take many forms such as a decline in caloric intake, malnutrition, ill-health accompanied by loss of income, or death. For example, individuals living in moderate and extreme poverty may be swayed or enticed to forego the purchase of basic goods for their families, harming the general physical and psychological capabilities necessary for human functioning.

Despite technological advances in agriculture and rising incomes, MEP households are consuming less food and survive on 1400 calories on average per person, roughly half of that needed for a healthy diet (Banerjee and Duflo 2011). Adult malnourishment adversely affects current daily activities, long-term welfare, and wages, while creating higher demand for medical care (Derose et al. 1998). Child malnourishment severely affects development, growth, cognitive ability, and occupational performance in adulthood (Chavez et al. 1995). Studies show that the MEP are not maximizing their caloric intake, often acting as if they are not malnourished by not spending more of their available income on extra food. According to Banerjee and Duflo (2007), unhealthy patterns of food, alcohol, and tobacco consumption amongst the MEP are quite common. In Mexico, for example, as high as 8.1% of the household's budget goes to alcohol and tobacco. Impoverished urban MEP consumers in China spend as much as 46% of income on tobacco (Liu et al. 2006).

An estimated 41.8 million Chinese fall into poverty because of excessive cigarette spending each year (Liu et al. 2006). Banerjee and Duflo (2011) point out that countries such as Mexico and India have seen an emergence in fast-moving consumer goods, oftentimes packaged in small sachets. The rising demand for such goods seems to correlate with falling food consumption. These behaviors are attributable to what Macarov (2003) describes as "norms, which are marked by very short term objectives and a live for the moment tendency" (p. 46). These studies underscore the critical trade-offs that MEP households make against providing necessities such as nourishment, education, and healthcare.

The vulnerability of the MEP is exacerbated by their inability to manage social and economic risks as a result of having limited access to assets (Alwang et al. 2001). When the MEP are sick or injured, or when crops fail, there is little recourse other than family, and typically no savings and no insurance to cover expenses or lost income. The higher an individual's placement among the economic tiers, the better an individual's ability to manage risk. The suscepti-bility of the MEP to harm as a result of their vulnerability is unique relative to other economic tiers for two reasons.

First, their lack of assets is significantly greater than those at higher tiers leading to a greater inability to manage risk than those in tiers 1–3. Second, the potential harmful outcomes of those in tier 4 are greater than those in tiers 1–3. Those living in moderate poverty are at direct risk of slipping into extreme poverty and suffering greater malnutrition and ill-health as a result. Those living in extreme poverty at tier 5 have little margin for reduced consumption and, as a result, are at risk of severe acute malnutrition and death.

Finally, those living in the range above $2 a day, but near that figure, will often experience similar vulnerability to those living in moderate poverty making the population of vulnerable poor larger than 2.6 billion. A person living on $1.95 a day and a person living on $2.25 a day, for example, are likely to experience similar cognitive and social vulnerability. The line between the MEP and the remainder of the BoP should not be understood as hard and fixed. Understanding the vulnerabilities of the MEP can help scholars and practitioners to better understand the vulnerabilities of the BoP in general.

In summary, the 2.6 billion people that comprise the MEP live in multidi-mensional poverty and are both cognitively and socially vulnerable. This vulner-ability contributes to them making sub-optimal purchasing decisions relative to their well-being, understood as the capacity to function well. Understanding this vulnerability will allow us to provide an account of the exploitation of the moderate and extremely poor and a theory of morally legitimate TNC ventures targeting these potential customers, producers, and workers.

An Empowerment Theory of Morally Legitimate BoP Ventures

In this section, several of the theoretical aspects of the BoP proposition are developed. A basic feature of the BoP proposition is the idea that BoP activities are morally legitimate. However, previous research on BoP activities has not provided an adequate theoretical basis for distinguishing between morally legitimate and morally illegitimate BoP activities. Moral legitimacy has been defined as "a positive normative evaluation of the organization and its activities" (Suchman 1995: 579). This section explains how BoP business ventures can be understood to be morally legitimate or morally illegitimate. To facilitate this theoretical development, an account of exploitation is provided, an interpretation of the meaning of "benefit" in the BoP proposition is provided, and an account of the relationship of the BoP proposition to human rights is defended.

Exploitation

At the core of entrepreneurial activity is the exploitation of opportunities (Casson 1982; Shane and Venkataraman 2000). BoP theorists argue that TNC managers neglect many opportunities because of "orthodoxies" in assumptions and practices (Prahalad and Hart 2002: 4) that lead them to neglect the BoP as a viable market. The "dominant logic" into which they have been socialized leads TNC managers to emphasize large unit packs, high margins per unit, and high volume sales (Prahalad 2004: 49). What has been missing in most TNCs are managers who can imagine alternative strategies that will allow them to exploit BoP populations with the aid and assistance of knowledgeable local experts. However, as noted above, BoP strategies have also been criticized precisely because they are exploitative (Karnani 2007; Santos and Laczniak 2009). This dispute over the moral legitimacy of exploitative entrepreneurial activity at the BoP points to a need for theoretical development of the ethical dimensions of BoP strategies. To advance understanding of the ethics of BoP strategies, it will be useful to clarify the role of exploitation at the BoP in general and of the 2.6 billion MEP in particular.

In ordinary language usage, it is common to refer to the utilization of a resource as exploitation. For example, one might exploit a hilltop vista to build a house or one might exploit a mineral deposit or a fishery for economic gain. In these cases, exploitation stands in for "use" and carries with it an amoral connotation. Let us refer to this as the *utilization* meaning of exploitation. In entrepreneurship, this use of the term is commonly employed in characterizing the identification and targeting of underutilized, previously unknown, or newly created, possibilities to create positive outcomes. In the case of BoP business ventures, the intended outcome is binary in that it is intended to be both positive for the TNC and for the customer. The benefit for the TNC is profits, but the precise benefit for BoP customers is not always clear in the literature. We will return to the issue of positive outcomes for BoP populations below.

The meaning of the negative use of the term, exploitation, invoked in discussions of BoP strategies remains unclear. However, the use is clearly intended to connote harm. Let us refer to this as the harm meaning of exploitation. Wood (1995) has defended the position that the exploitation of people (as opposed to nature) always involves one party taking advantage of the weakness or vulnerability of another party (Arnold 2003a). However, taking advantage of the vulnerable should be understood as a necessary condition rather than a sufficient condition for exploitation. In market economies, entrepreneurial firms routinely take advantages of the vulnerabilities of competitors to exploit market opportunities, and this is commonly regarded as legitimate business activity. But when is exploitation morally wrong? Exploitation may be understood as wrong when it fails to respect human rights, especially basic human rights.

Human Rights and International Business

Human rights theory play an important role in international business ethics and corporate social responsibility since Donaldson (1991) provided a theory of TNC human rights duties (Arnold 2010, 2013; Campbell 2006; Cragg 2002; Cragg et al. 2012; Kobrin 2009; Wettstein 2012a, 2012b). The TNC duty to respect human rights has a two-fold ethical justification. First, human rights are grounded in the idea that agency, or the capacity of autonomous action, is worthy of respect and that individual persons should be respected by those persons or organizations with whom they have relationships (Arnold 2010). In the case of TNCs, this includes relationships with customers, as well as other stakeholders such as employees.

Second, TNC human rights duties are defended on contractualist grounds (Donaldson 1991; Cragg 2002). Here, the argument is that the very reason that corporations are permitted to exist is to allow people to come together to make productive contributions to society. To accomplish this, end corporations are granted such rights as property, ownership, and freedom. In virtue of being granted these rights, corporations have reciprocal duties to respect the rights of others, including the basic human rights enjoyed by real persons. These two arguments are compatible and together provide an overlapping justification for the view that corporations operating in different nations have a duty to respect human rights independently of the ability of host-nation governments to police and remedy human rights violations.

The adoption or endorsement of human rights norms for business by the United Nations (UN) and other global civil society organizations and the attendant adaptation and endorsement of human rights duties for TNCs by many companies themselves are important trends in international business ethics. In 2011, the United Nations Human Rights Council endorsed a new set of global guiding principles for business: the UN "Protect, Respect and

Remedy" Framework. The UN Framework calls upon business enterprises to respect the rights of all persons and to provide remedy when those rights are violated (Ruggie 2008). The UN Framework is itself an extension and articulation of elements of the UN Global Compact, a strategic policy initiative for businesses that facilitates the incorporation of ten universally accepted moral principles into business policy. Firms gain moral legitimacy when they act in a manner consistent with justified international human rights norms.

Many businesses highlighted in BoP case studies, such as CEMEX, Coca-Cola, ITC, and Unilever, are among the over 8700 current business participants in the Global Compact. The specific human rights that the UN Framework calls upon businesses to respect, and those to which signatories of the Global Compact have pledged to accept, are those included in the International Bill of Human Rights (which includes the Universal Declaration). Among these rights is Article 25 (1) of the Universal Declaration, which states in part that "Everyone has the right to a standard of living adequate for the health and well-being of himself and of his family, including food, clothing, housing and medical care and necessary social services" (1948).

MEP populations live in deprivation of the human rights to subsistence and well-being, and this deprivation undermines their ability to exercise other rights (Shue 1996; Sen 2009). Capabilities are needed to attain subsistence and the ability to function well is necessary for the attainment of well-being. Business ventures may either enhance or inhibit human capabilities to function well.

Harmful exploitation of MEP populations occurs when TNCs take advantage of the cognitive and social vulnerabilities of the MEP in ways that violate or undermine their human rights. Such exploitation is an example of morally illegitimate TNC activity. This account has the advantage of explaining morally illegitimate ventures targeting the MEP, as well as allowing for morally legitimate ventures targeting the MEP. However, further analysis is needed to provide a more fully realized theory of morally legitimate TNC ventures targeting the MEP.

Utility

Products and services marketed to the BoP may either improve the welfare of individuals or it may exacerbate the poverty of individuals. For example, affordable clean energy sources for a community may improve health and living standards. Companies such as D. Light are bringing clean energy through the sale of solar-powered LED lanterns into BoP markets in rural India (Shukla and Bairiganjan 2011). However, tobacco products will typically cause a decline in welfare by harming health and diverting money from basic needs. As we noted in the introduction, an essential feature of BoP ventures is the promise of benefitting BoP populations. There are at least two ways of characterizing the benefits to BoP populations in general, and the MEP in particular, that business ventures may bring: increased utility through the satisfaction of desires, or increased achievement of human rights via the capacity to function well (Sen 1999). Clarifying these two ways in which the benefits to consumers may be assessed will provide us with additional conceptual tools for building a theory of morally legitimate TNC ventures that target the moderate and extreme poor.

Consider utility enhancement first, focusing on the MEP. With regard to food or consumer goods, for example, more choices can be seen as enhancing the possibility of utility satisfaction. An MEP consumer, in this view, is made better off by being presented with more opportunities to choose from in the marketplace (Prahalad 2004; Ireland 2008). For example, shops stocked with candy or sweets, tobacco products, sugary carbonated beverages, alcohol, skin whitening cream such as Unilever's controversial Fair and Lovely product, and lottery tickets provide the poor with more opportunities to satisfy desires. To the extent that the satisfaction of desires is the end, then the benefits of the product will be determined by the market demand among the MEP. Business ventures that tailor alcohol or tobacco products to the MEP, for example, and are rewarded with increased revenues, benefit the MEP on the utility view. Sales might be expanded, for example, by increasing the alcohol content of beer using local ingredients while reducing the volume per unit to reduce costs, or by adding to the nicotine content of the lowest grade tobacco to increase repeat sales and selling cigarettes in packs with fewer cigarettes to lower the price.

To illustrate the inadequacy of the utility view, consider the case of The Coca-Cola Company (TCCC) in Uganda. TCCC has developed a network of micro-distribution centers (MDC's) in African BoP markets that generate annual revenues in excess of $550 million (Business Call to Action 2008). TCCC relies on the MDC model as its main distribution channel in Uganda. Studies confirm that the MEP spend significant portions of their income on sugary products (Gordon 2007; Banerjee and Duflo 2007). However, there are at least two problems with targeting the MEP as new Coca-Cola consumers. First, there is a lack of relevant disposable income to consume the product in the first place; 17.6 million Ugandans are MEP consumers, yielding between $1.50 and $3.50 of free monthly cash flow after accounting for expenditures on necessities such as food, housing, water, and education (Hammond et al. 2007). Ugandans in this category would have to make important trade-offs in order to regularly consume Coca-Cola.

These trade-offs are pronounced when we consider that the data shows that the same group spends between $3.00 and $4.50 on housing and between $1.75 and $2.92 on water on a monthly basis. Depending on local price, the purchase of a single Coca-Cola beverage can represent 10–30% of a Ugandan's monthly housing and water expense alone. From a capabilities perspective, Coca-Cola is not in the best interest of MEP consumers in Uganda even though they are able to buy the product (Hammond et al. 2007).

Second, Heller et al. (2001) found significant associations between soda consumption and dental caries among individuals over 25 in the United States, the world's richest nation. Dental caries among individuals under 25, however, are not significantly correlated with soda consumption in the United States. The authors attribute the difference to the widespread use of fluorides since the 1960s. In BoP markets, the poor are more likely to suffer from high levels of dental caries because of the limited use of fluorides and lack of dental hygiene from a young age. A South African study found that parents "visit a dentist only when the child is symptomatic" (Gordon 2007: 183). Using health services only when emergency symptoms arise is typical in a BoP setting. In fact, 97% of Ugandans spend just $1.25 to $7.25 per month on health services (Hammond et al. 2007), suggesting that due to limited incomes overall, consumers behave reactively rather than proactively. In summary, while MEP consumers will purchase Coca-Cola products, the consumption of those products will divert income from more basic needs and contribute to poor health.

As this example illustrates, increasing the consumer choices of vulnerable populations does not always improve well-being and may contribute to a reduction in well-being. More consumer choices, accompanied by marketing, may lead individuals in circumstances of dire poverty to purchase alcohol products rather than millet, or accept usurious loan terms from a commercial micro-lender in order to celebrate a religious festival. Utility reflects a person's current mental state, and current mental states often do not take into account future states of affairs. In the case of MEP consumers, mental states are shaped by mal-nourishment, the hardship of living without basic goods such as running water, electricity, or sanitation, feelings of social estrangement, and the emotional consequences of losing family members to disease, starvation, or fatal injuries while laboring. The cognitive and social vulnerability of individuals living in the MEP provide them with reasons for making consumer choices that are not consistent with their ability to function well. Based on the foregoing analysis, we conclude that enhanced utility does not always benefit the MEP and sometimes results in harm to the MEP.

Capabilities

A second way of characterizing the benefits of ventures targeting the MEP is in terms of their ability to provide opportunities that enhance the capabilities of the MEP to function well as human beings. The capabilities approach is "a species of a human rights approach" and has been employed by the United Nations Development Program in its annual development reports since the 1990s in order to evaluate the attainment of human rights (Nussbaum 2007: 21; see also Sen 2005). The capabilities approach is a philosophical framework that emphasizes the importance of human functionings to well-being and stresses the importance of the capability to function well in allowing humans to maximize their well-being (Sen 1993, 1999, 2005, 2009).

To function well is to engage in activities and to experience states that a person would have reason to value. Examples of activities include walking, reading, thinking, artistic expression, income generation, or political participation. Examples of states include being well-nourished, not being ashamed of one's poverty, being pleased for one's children, and having self-respect. A capabilities approach differs from other measures of well-being, such as utility, by taking account of the range of conditions that impact the ability of individuals to function well as human beings. It is the capability to function well that allows us to reach our human potential.

Utilizing a capabilities framework, benefits to the MEP can usefully be distinguished into two different categories. First, ventures that provide opportunities for the MEP to improve their capability to function well constitute capabilities empowerment. These opportunities may take the form of employment, purchasing MEP products, or providing entrepreneurial opportunities. They are characterized by the opportunity they present for individuals in the MEP to utilize their labor to improve their capability to function well by earning income, growing food, securing their legal rights, or insuring them against risk. For example, an agribusiness company that provided seed and fertilizer on an installment plan and delivered it to the purchaser would enhance the capability of farmers and their families to function well by better enabling them to grow crops for subsistence and for sale at market. Similarly, a company that provided the farmer with the means to secure legal title to his land, or to insure him against crop failure, would enhance the ability of the farmer and his family to function well.

Second, an MEP consumer may be benefitted by ventures that offer direct opportunities for them to function well by purchasing products or services, the use of which directly improves their well-being and which constitute *functionings empowerment*. For example, forests near population centers throughout the world are being depleted for cooking fuel used in rural homes. The emissions are a health hazard and the gathering of fuel negatively impacts local ecosystems. A company that sold affordable, reliable, and durable solar concentration cookers would provide an opportunity for MEP households to improve health conditions and reduce time spent gathering wood. With both types of empowerment, it may be necessary for TNCs to engage in education of MEP populations regarding the advantages of the opportunities provided in order to facilitate adaptation. Based on the foregoing analysis, business ventures benefit the MEP when they provide capabilities empowerment or functionings empowerment.

Exploitation Versus Empowerment

Business ventures that take advantage of the cognitive and social vulnerability of the MEP in ways that fail to respect their human rights are morally objectionable even though they may be profitable. Our earlier examination of the capabilities approach to poverty sheds light on when products or services can support human rights such as subsistence and well-being that are of particular relevance when addressing poverty. Business ventures that negatively impact capabilities and functioning undermine human rights, whereas ventures that positively impact capabilities and functioning support human rights. From an ethical perspective, TNCs wrongfully exploit the MEP if their business ventures undermine basic human rights such as subsistence and well-being. As we have seen, human rights norms are increasingly accepted as a basis for the normative evaluation of TNC activities. On this analysis, firms that target the BoP do so in a morally legitimate manner when they support the attainment of human rights.

The MEP struggle for survival and aspire to attain better lives for themselves and their children. Utilizing the theoretical framework developed in this chapter, the ethical dimensions of MEP business ventures fall into one of two categories: exploitation strategies or empowerment strategies (see Figure 7.2 below). Exploitation strategies take advantage of the vulnerability of MEP populations to advance the interests of the firm without providing empowerment for the consumer and potentially harming the consumer.

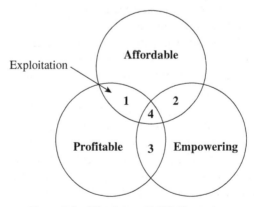

Figure 7.2   Typology of MEP Strategies.

Successful exploitation strategies are affordable in the sense that MEP consumers can purchase the good or service at a price that results in profits for the TNC, even if they must sacrifice basic necessities such as food for themselves or their families in order to purchase the product or service. Such ventures may be characterized as win–lose scenarios where the TNC wins in the form of profits and the MEP loses in terms of capabilities or functioning (See Figure 7.2: 1). As we have detailed, the case of TCCC is an example of a win–lose scenario. TCCC has generated substantial profits while negatively impacting capabilities and functionings. (A detailed account of the potential exploitation of BoP workers and producers is beyond the scope of this chapter. For discussion of the exploitation of workers, see Arnold 2003b and Arnold 2009.)

Empowerment strategies take the form of capabilities empowerment or functionings empowerment and facilitate the attainment of human rights such as subsistence and well-being. Empowerment strategies are not necessarily affordable for the MEP consumer or profitable for the TNC. When the venture contributes to capabilities empowerment or functionings empowerment, but its products or services cannot be made affordable (see Figure 7.2: 3), the venture fails as an MEP venture. Hindustan Lever, Limited (HLL), a subsidiary of the consumer products giant, Unilever, has been operating in BoP markets for many years. Like TCCC, their size and scale in BoP markets are among the largest in this category of TNCs.

Annapurna Salt is a technological innovation brought to market by HLL that has clear benefits for the MEP in BoP markets (Rajendrah and Shah 2003). This specially formulated salt retains iodine at a significantly higher rate than other branded and unbranded salts and can positively impact iodine deficiency disorder (IDD), a serious health problem in many BoP markets. From a capabilities perspective, reducing mental defects among children and adults through salt consumption has the potential to allow millions to avoid IDD and realize their human potential. However, despite convincing research in support of the product and the marketing prowess of Unilever, Ireland (2008) shows that Annapurna Salt never achieved more than 10% market share; and the distribution channel made up of women in rural Indian villages, known as Project Shakti, reached a head count of just 12 000 despite HLL's projection of over 500 000. Weidner et al. (2010) cites the lack of financial success of Project Shakti and the high turnover rate of the women entrepreneurs, known as Shakti Ammas ("strong mothers"). Karnani (2007) shows that Annapurna Salt was simply too expensive at a price premium of 275% relative to available brands. Like many beneficial pharmaceutical and consumer products that require large investments in R&D to bring to market, Annapurna Salt could not be profitable by selling only to MEP consumers because the product is largely unaffordable for this segment. For this reason, HLL has positioned Annapurna Salt for wealthier segments of developing markets with greater success.

The corollary outcome is one where the price for the product or service is made affordable but where the revenues are insufficient to make the product or service profitable (See Figure 7.2: 2). To illustrate the corollary scenario, consider the case of Procter & Gamble (P&G). In 2003, P&G embarked on an ambitious project to bring a water purification product (PuR) to BoP markets (Hanson and Powell 2006). Armed with the knowledge that inadequate sanitation kills millions of MEP consumers each year, they invested $20 million in marketing and research and development from 1995 to 2003, including three years of market tests to ensure the product met customer needs.

Water is used for drinking, cooking, and personal hygiene. When contaminated, it represents a dangerous mechanism for the transmission of disease. From a capabilities and human rights perspective, safe access to clean drinking water is an element of the basic human right to subsistence. The human body requires a minimum amount of water to survive. Contaminated water presents a drain on household resources, as family members often have to travel long distances to obtain water and spend an inordinate amount of time caring for sick household members who contract a variety of diseases. Having clean water would help MEP consumers utilize their time for more productive tasks that help them attain critical functionings to live well. Therefore, solving this problem represents a unique opportunity for P&G.

PuR sachets were proven to reduce diarrheal disease by 20–90% with an average reduction of 50%. Despite this promise, a cheaper (though less effective) bleach alternative existed in the market. "Although consumer research suggested that PuR was affordable to the consumer, at US$0.01 per liter it was still regarded as relatively expensive as a household water treatment strategy" (Hanson and Powell 2006: 9). Even though PuR was affordable for MEP consumers, the product experienced low customer retention rates from competitive forces. As a result, P&G was not able to generate the revenue necessary to be profitable in the long term or recoup start-up costs in the short term. Lose–win scenarios are unsustainable as business policy, but they may be candidates for charitable activity or for partnerships with nongovernmental organizations or government agencies. Despite being unprofitable, P&G continued the PuR project on a charitable basis because of the significant benefit it brought to BoP markets.

Finally, ventures that empower the MEP, and are both affordable and profitable, may be characterized as win–win scenarios (See Figure 7.2: 4). Such ventures should be the goal of TNCs that aspire to do well by doing good while serving the MEP. The most far-reaching win–win business ventures present in BoP markets involve wireless information and communication technology (ICT).

Mobile telephony leads to functionings empowerment in a number of ways. The emergence of thousands of "phone ladies" and shopkeepers is an entrepreneurial benefit for communities providing new income sources. Access to mobile phone communications provides rural villagers with the ability to learn about market prices for commodities, contact health care professionals and government authorities more quickly, and maintain relationships with family members who have migrated. ICT has a multitude of ancillary uses aside from person-to-person communication. The adaptability of the technology is making it easier for MEP consumers to bank, communicate, trade, and obtain weather forecasts. Companies like Voxiva are using the scalability of ITC to communicate health alerts and prevent epidemics in remote villages. Microfinance institutions like Grameen Bank are using ICT to deliver banking services. TNCs like ITC Limited (ITC) are using the power of ICT devices to integrate their supply chain with rural farmers through programs like ITC's e-Choupal (2011). Through ICT, MEP consumers can improve their ability to function well.

From an affordability perspective, the low cost to manufacture simple handsets have played a major role in the success of ICT. As village shopkeepers have shown, the upfront cost can be reduced or possibly eliminated when the phone is used as a productive asset. For the TNCs involved, profit margins can be substantial. Subscribers in developing countries worldwide grew fivefold between 2000 and 2005 to 1.4 billion users (Hammond et al. 2007). Telenor AG maintains margins between 40 and 50% and has over 30 million subscribers (Malaviya et al. 2004). Celtel holds 28% of the market in Nigeria with 8 million subscribers with $888 million in revenues in 2006 at a gross margin of 36.3% (Anderson et al. 2010). These examples illustrate that mobile telephony as an example of a win–win scenario at the BoP.

Multi-Stage BoP Opportunity Assessment Process

Given the identification of the four distinct outcomes that BoP business models can generate, we are now in a position to identify a multi-stage opportunity assessment process for TNC ventures that target the MEP to aid them in achieving moral legitimacy as they seek to form profitable ventures. Figure 7.3 illustrates this process.

The first stage in our assessment process involves the evaluation of entrepreneurial opportunities in the context of BoP Markets. Prahalad (2004) cites increasing competition and slowing growth in developed economies as motivating factors for TNCs to consider BoP markets. McMullen and Shepherd (2006) argue that prior knowledge and general motivation can result in the belief that entrepreneurial opportunities exist in a market. For example, a TNC may see opportunities via awareness of problems such as unsanitary water, disease, malnutrition, and a lack of financial services in BoP markets and ask, "What can be done about this?" If the TNC determines that an opportunity exists, a belief in a third-party opportunity forms. By themselves, third-party

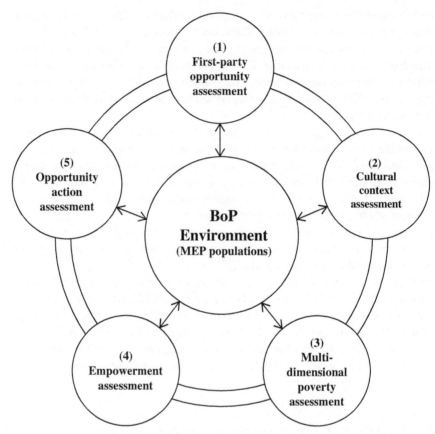

Figure 7.3   Multi-Stage BoP Opportunity Assessment Process.

opportunities are not enough for a TNC to take action in the market because specific knowledge and motivation to exploit these opportunities may not exist within the firm. TNC managers must believe an opportunity exists for the firm, thereby creating a first-party opportunity. An assessment of the firm's knowledge (feasibility assessment) and motivation (desirability assessment) related to third-party opportunities must take place before a belief in a third-party opportunity can be transformed into a first-party opportunity.

The assessment process involved in forming a first-party opportunity begins with the acquisition of more knowledge by utilizing a consultant or assigning a task force of firm employees to look into the opportunity while assessing the potential risks and rewards. Before a firm can develop strategic intent (Hamel and Prahalad 1989), assemble resources, form strategies, and penetrate markets, it must first form beliefs about the opportunities it sees in the market. Entrepreneurial opportunities in BoP markets with high MEP populations differ from other market opportunities, however, because they are closely related to problems associated with social and cognitive vulnerabilities in the context of pervasive poverty. For first-party opportunities to be morally legitimate, they must at least have the potential to empower MEP consumers and support their basic human rights.

The second stage in the assessment process involves understanding the circumstances of the MEP population being targeted in order to gain a clear assessment of the market opportunity. Attention to the importance of local context has received increased attention from international management scholars in recent years (Meyer et al. 2011). The special circumstances of MEP populations will depend upon the context of each culture and the uniqueness of a particular country or region. For example, the MEP in Brazil primarily live in densely populated urban centers, whereas the MEP in Bangladesh are widely dispersed in rural villages.

Grameenphone's partnership with Telenor illustrates the importance of local context (Malaviya et al. 2004). In order to penetrate rural markets in Bangladesh, Grameenphone pioneered the village phone concept. Individually, the poor in Bangladesh could not afford mobile phones; but collectively, each person could afford to pay for a small amount of usage. To implement the idea, Grameenphone developed the role of the "village phone lady," a village woman who would become a local merchant of Grameenphone services. Similarly, microfinance institutions, such as Grameen Bank, focus their services on rural women. Through these models, women become empowered and receive opportunities to improve their capability to function well. The practice of focusing on women emerges from a unique understanding of local context and local culture. Understanding these local contexts will help TNCs assess the community-level characteristics of the markets where they see promising first-party opportunities.

The third part of the assessment procedure concerns the multidimensionality of poverty. In addition to local context, unique dimensions and varying intensities of poverty exist in different settings. The academic and development communities have made significant progress in providing robust data on dimensions such as health, education, and living standards in recent years for many regions and countries. As more data has emerged, the United Nations Development Programme (UNDP) released the Human Poverty Index (HPI) in 2007, which laid the groundwork for a more robust Multidimensional Poverty Index (MPI) released in 2010. This index takes into account health, education, and living standards as central poverty dimensions. Altogether, the three dimensions are supported by ten poverty indicators provide an overview of the intensity of poverty not previously attained by monetary approaches. The indicators provided in the MPI are not intended to be a definitive and final list, but instead reflect data that can be measured and is widely available.

An understanding of multidimensional poverty is important for three reasons. First, indexes like the MPI and HPI give TNCs tools to assess the efficacy of first-party opportunities. TNCs gain the ability to more accurately decipher the poverty alleviation potential of a perceived BoP opportunity. BoP opportunities that are potentially harmful to the well-being of the MEP should not extend beyond the opportunity assessment stages of this process. Second, TNCs can create specific poverty alleviation goals that will assist them in designing social value propositions during the planning stages of the venture.

Poverty alleviation goals are closely linked to our characterization of capabilities and functionings empowerment. Where TNCs engage in capabilities and functionings empowerment in MEP populations, they also engage in poverty alleviation, and thus, morally legitimate business activity. The MPI and HPI provide important matrices for TNCs to embed social value creation as a fundamental function to every step of the venture formation process. Third, multidimensional indicators can be used to predict the impact of a given business strategy before it has been launched. These predictions can they be used to assess impact after the strategy has been implemented. As a result, TNCs will be in a better position to increase total wealth through the combination of economic value creation and social value creation (Zahra et al. 2009) while continuing to monitor and reassess their strategy where necessary.

The fourth stage of the assessment process involves an appraisal of whether or not there is an opportunity to facilitate capabilities empowerment or functionings empowerment. Here, TNCs managers explicitly focus on the ways that the potential product or service will engage the MEP given what they have learned in previous stages. TNCs that aim to give MEP populations an opportunity to improve their capabilities to function well will gather information on how they can employ the poor, provide them with entrepreneurial opportunities, or purchase goods directly from them. For example, SC Johnson found a way to integrate pyrethrum farmers in Kenya into their supply chain (World Business Council for Sustainable Development 2004). By partnering with the Pyrethrum Board of Kenya, they were able to establish a market to purchase goods directly from the poor, thereby improving their income. TNCs that aim to facilitate functionings empowerment can gather information on how their potential products and services may provide opportunities for the poor to function well. For example, Danone began offering yogurt supplements that provided the MEP with fortified drinks to benefit growth and development in African BoP markets where malnourishment is common (Hawarden and Barnard 2011).

Throughout this stage, as TNCs sketch out potential product prototypes or services, they can make a realistic appraisal of the unique social and economic value the product or service has the potential to bring. TNCs can do this by using their knowledge of local contexts to produce lists of the types of capabilities and functionings that would help the MEP live better lives. In this respect, each country, region, and culture will present unique challenges and deficiencies. TNC managers must ask three important questions at this stage of the process. First, "What capabilities and functionings is our product or service likely to support?" Second, "How might the potential product or service contribute to these capabilities and functionings?" Third, "How might the potential product or service undermine these capabilities and functionings?" Considering whether or not the product can have meaningful social and economic value must be done realistically. No TNC can improve all deficiencies in capabilities and functionings, nor should we expect them to. What is important is that TNCs gather information on whether their potential product or service will impact or degrade capabilities and functionings. As we have established, TNCs can achieve moral legitimacy when their products and services empower the MEP, but may reasonably be regarded as acting illegitimately when their business ventures wrongfully exploit the MEP. At this stage of the decision procedure, ventures that are determined to be exploitative rather than empowering can be identified and abandoned.

The final stage of the process is the opportunity action assessment. One of the essential contributions entrepreneurship has made to broader business and economic theory is in the "examination of how, by whom, and with what effects opportunities to create future goods and services are discovered, evaluated, and exploited" (Shane and Venkataraman 2000: 218). The first four stages of the assessment process focus on the evaluation of entrepreneurial opportunities through an ethical lens.

This stage of the entrepreneurial process is important because it is an antecedent to successful entrepreneurial action. Here firms ask, "How can we bring forth this potentially empowering product or service at this cost?" As this stage TNC managers will make cost projections and develop context-specific distribution and promotion strategies. London and Hart (2004) describe successful strategies that center around collaborating with nontraditional partners and building local capacity.

In conclusion, the multi-stage assessment process gives TNCs the ability to assess morally legitimate first-party business opportunities that can be exploited on the premise that both economic and social gain will result. This is accomplished through the extensive gathering of information related to culture, multidimensional poverty, capabilities, and functionings. At each stage, TNCs have the chance to look at ways to empower the MEP while systematically ruling out the opportunities that can wrongfully exploit the MEP. If TNCs assess BoP markets through an ethical lens, they ensure that the "doing good" component of business ventures targeting the MEP is investigated with similar rigor and attention as the "doing well" component. Our analysis has focused on the social dimensions of poverty, but the environmental impact of firm activities on the BoP will also need to be assessed before a complete assessment of a firm's impact on the TNC can be assessed (Arnold and Williams 2012).

Instrumental Versus Ethical Corporate Social Responsibility

Morally legitimate business ventures that target the MEP should result in profitability for the firm and empowerment for members of the MEP, rather than harmful exploitation. Our conclusions have significant implications for theories of corporate social responsibility.

Instrumental, or economic, corporate social responsibility holds that corporations should engage in pro-social or ethical conduct beyond what is required by law, only when doing so will improve the return on investment of the financiers of the organization (Gond et al. 2009); McWilliams and Siegel 2001; McWilliams et al. 2006). The term "instrumental" CSR is more appropriate than the term "economic" CSR because it better reflects the idea that the exclusive duty or obligation of managers is to promote shareholder, or financier, wealth within the law, regardless of other ethical considerations. In this sense, pro-social behavior is of instrumental value to shareholders or financiers. On the other hand, the term "economic" refers to a much broader domain of concern and might include, for example, considerations regarding public welfare beyond the narrow interests of shareholders or financiers. In this view, the role of managers regarding CSR is to engage in ongoing cost-benefit analysis that balances the claims and expectations of various stakeholders (both internal and external) against firm profitability. Meeting increased stakeholder expectations will sometimes result in greater demand and improved revenues. According to the instrumental CSR position, in such cases the additional cost of CSR is justified because of increased revenues. However, CSR initiatives that do not increase revenues are not justified and should not be undertaken.

Defenders of the BoP proposition have yet to introduce into the literature empirical data to support the conclusion that a TNCs failure to serve the BoP will result in reputational losses that will, in turn, lead to reduced revenues or profitability. However, from the perspective of instrumental CSR, if such external pressure on a firm were determined to be a threat to profitability, any business venture targeting the MEP that relieved the external pressure would be justified regardless of whether or not it exploited or empowered MEP populations.

Regardless of external pressure, from the perspective of instrumental CSR, any venture targeting the MEP that can be made profitable should be undertaken unless there is a clear expectation that undertaking the initiative will result in an overall reduction in firm profitability or the opportunity cost of operating in an environment, such as the BoP, exceeds the return of another investment elsewhere. On this account of CSR, both empowerment strategies and exploitation strategies should be undertaken when profitable. If one strategy is more profitable than the other strategy, then it should be pursued. In this view, the harmful exploitation of the world's poorest populations is a normative requirement for socially responsible firms whenever it is profitable.

That is, firms should engage in harmful exploitation whenever doing so is profitable. Ethical considerations, such as respect for basic human rights, are not relevant to TNC strategy development for its own sake, or out of consideration for related ethical values such as respect for persons or human dignity, on an instrumental conception of CSR.

There are at least two possible explanations as to why proponents of the instrumental conception of CSR may believe this is the case. First, advocates of this view may presume that a robust regulatory environment and social services for the MEP and other BoP segments are available as is the case in many developed nations. Operating with such an assumption, it may be presumed to be the role of governments to protect the vulnerable from the hardships of poverty. However, it is well understood that resource scarcity, corruption, and institutional failures in many developing nations help ensure that the MEP receive little in the way of governmental protection or services. A second explanation is that proponents of the instrumental model of CSR believe that the fiduciary duty of managers to TNC shareholders always outweigh competing ethical obligations to other parties. On this conception of CSR, the economic value of wealth creation for shareholders always supersedes consideration of other values such as basic human rights. In order for this position to be viable, proponents of the instrumental view of CSR need to explain why the agent-based and social contract-based arguments supporting basic human rights duties or responsibilities (discussed above) for corporations fail or are superseded by obligations to shareholders.

The idea of corporate irresponsibility may also be utilized in evaluating the implications of the instrumental model of CSR regarding ventures targeting the MEP. Armstrong defines corporate irresponsibility as "a decision to accept an alternative that is thought by the decision makers to be inferior to another alternative when the effects upon all parties are considered" (Armstrong 1977: 185). On Armstrong's account of corporate irresponsibility, the effects of decisions regarding the MEP may impact both wealth creation for shareholders and the capability of the MEP to function well. According to the analysis provided above, a firm that engages in exploitation strategies when targeting the MEP will cause them to be worse off *ex post* than they would have been had the venture not been undertaken. On the instrumental model of corporate social responsibility, this harmful outcome is justified whenever doing so will enhance shareholder wealth. If the harm to the MEP caused by the exploitative strategy is taken to be significant, this may be regarded on Armstrong's account as an example of corporate irresponsibility. Paradoxically, then, the instrumental view of corporate responsibility may require actions that constitute corporate irresponsibility.

This apparent inconsistency points to the need for an account of CSR that accommodates values or ends other than wealth enhancement for shareholders. According to Windsor, an ethical account of corporate social responsibility maintains that TNCs should practice "broad self-restraint and altruism" in order to take into account values other than wealth enhancement for shareholders (Windsor 2006: 98; see also McWilliams et al. 2006). However, Windsor does not defend a particular set of norms that can be utilized to establish a framework for corporate policy that will serve as a basis for determining when self-restraint is appropriate and when it is not.

We can begin to partially fill in an account of ethical CSR by noting that the expectations regarding the ability of TNC managers to exercise self-restraint apply to both the instrumental and the ethical conceptions of CSR. To see this, let us first note that TNCs operate in multiple regulatory environments with different laws and regulations and varied enforcement capacities. In many jurisdictions, the enforcement of many laws and regulations are lax or nonexistent. TNCs that adhere to the instrumental model of CSR must exercise self-restraint in such contexts in order to adhere to the law, even when violating the law would be more profitable. Even if such self-restraint with respect to the law is exercised, opportunities for the legal exploitation of the MEP abound. When confronted with opportunities to pursue profitable exploitation strategies of the MEP, TNCs that adhere to an ethical model of CSR will exhibit similar self-restraint in order to avoid harming the poor at the BoP. Both conceptions of CSR share the assumption that managers are capable of guiding corporate behavior based on considerations other than mere profit maximization and should do so despite potential losses for shareholders.

Sound ethical reasons support respecting basic human rights grounded in conceptions of human agency and in social contract theory, thousands of companies have committed to respecting human rights, and international treaties and conventions have endorsed the position that TNCs have a responsibility to respect basic human rights. Taken together, these provide good reasons for believing that one element of ethical CSR should be respect for basic human rights and that TNCs should exhibit self-restraint to avoid violating or undermining such rights. The role of human rights in ethical CSR is best understood as a side-constraint on economic activity.

The pursuit of shareholder wealth is to be pursued via strategies and practices that respect basic ethical norms. TNCs operating in a global business environment have a particular need for universally binding side-constraints given the multitude of environments in which they operate, and respect for human rights constitutes an appropriate ethical constraint on business activity. This is not to claim that TNCs have a duty to supersede governments or to act as charitable organizations in enhancing the attainment of human rights. The claim defended here is that when they engage in business ventures, TNCs have a duty to respect the human rights of those with whom they have business relationships.

The logic of the instrumental conception of CSR leads to the conclusion that disrespecting impoverished individuals by exploiting their vulnerability and undermining their basic human rights is a duty of managers whenever doing do so is profitable. But the economic value of shareholder wealth creation is only one of the values that is relevant to a fully realized theory of CSR. Other values are relevant as well, and one such value is that of respect for basic human rights.

Conclusions

When TNCs engage the MEP as customers, they should support the attainment of human rights in the goods or services that they provide. However, the arguments of this paper do not support the stronger conclusion that the TNCs have a duty to undertake ventures on their own that serve the MEP (or the BOP) as customers. TNCs have different competencies, experience, and knowledge of different markets. Not all TNCs are well situated to serve the MEP market. Some TNCs may be in a better position to partner with NGOs and governments to bring appropriate technology, such as basic health care, running water, electricity, or improved sanitation, to the MEP. Other TNCs competencies may lead them to forgo engagement with the MEP altogether. It is when TNCs do target the MEP as a market that the duty to support human rights via capabilities and functionings empowerment is applicable. In this sense, the duty to promote MEP empowerment is not merely an instrumental response to external pressure by civil society but a binding duty, the fulfillment of which carries with it moral legitimacy. The duty to respect human rights is applicable in the context of relationships TNCs have with consumers or producers, but the duty does not arise independently of such relationships.

New TNC business ventures that target the MEP should be grounded in an awareness of the ability of a product or service to enhance capabilities or functionings in the particular cultural context of specific developing nations. Ventures that do not have a clear potential to empower the poor, but instead undermine the ability of the poor to achieve basic human rights, may be legitimately characterized as wrongfully exploitative based on the foregoing analysis. The promise of business ventures directed at the MEP and other BoP segments is not that of increased consumption leading to dignity, it is that of specialized products and services, as well as labor and production opportunities, empowering individuals to live more fully human lives and thereby supporting the attainment of basic human rights. Because instrumental CSR cannot accommodate this conclusion, it should be rejected as an inadequate theory of CSR.

Chapter Eight

The Paradox at the Base of the Pyramid: Environmental Sustainability and Market-Driven Poverty Alleviation

The scientific community warns that the Earth is facing an environmental crisis because of historical patterns of consumption and waste in production typical in the United States and other industrialized economies (Wackernagel et al. 2002). These negative environmental impacts will have a disproportionately harmful impact on the base of the pyramid (BoP) populations. If TNC business strategies contribute to environmental degradation, then serving the social needs of the world's poor may undermine the integrity of the natural environments they inhabit and actually harm them. We provide an analysis of the BoP proposition that gives equal weight to ethical considerations regarding environmental harms and strategic considerations regarding the exploitation of BoP markets. In the first part of this chapter, we provide a conceptual framework for understanding the environmental harms that transnational corporations (TNCs) and other business organizations can have on the BoP. Next, we identify the paradox of BoP business strategies in relation to environmental sustainability and offer a business policy-based resolution to the paradox that is consistent with the logic of the BoP proposition.

In the previous chapter, we argued that some BoP ventures may negatively impact human capabilities and functioning and thereby undermine the attainment of the basic human rights of moderately and extremely poor populations (2012). We argued that such "exploitation strategies" take advantage of the vulnerability of the moderately and extremely poor (MEP) in order to advance firm interests without providing empowerment for the consumer and potentially harming the consumer. We distinguished such strategies from "empowerment strategies" that facilitate the attainment of human rights such as subsistence and well-being. Our arguments show that profitable ventures that

The Ethics of Global Business, First Edition. Denis G. Arnold.
© 2023 John Wiley & Sons Ltd. Published 2023 by John Wiley & Sons Ltd.

serve the BoP do not necessarily improve the lives of the BoP. Profit remains the primary incentive for companies to seek out the BoP market according to many scholars. Poverty alleviation is the desirable effect of BoP strategies but not the main goal (Gardetti and D'Andrea 2010; Landrum 2007). Our analysis in this chapter covers ventures that target the BoP in any capacity, whether as consumer or producer, with emphasis on the fact that the BoP is being targeted for profit motives.

Environmental Impacts at the Base of the Pyramid

A tension or conflict between increased consumption at the BoP and environmental protection has been noted from the outset (Prahalad and Hart 2002). For example, the increased sale of single-serve size products, including beverages, shampoo, and other personal care products, tea, and medicine, creates increased waste (Karnani 2007; Prahalad 2004; Prahalad and Hart 2002). The solution that has been proposed since the BoP proposition was introduced has been to stipulate that BoP initiatives should be environmentally sustainable (Prahalad and Hart 2002, p. 2; Prahalad 2004, p. 57). For example, Prahalad and Hart cite the need for a reduction in resource intensity, an increase in recyclability, and more use of renewable energy (2002, p. 6). There are at least three problems with this response. First, it is not clear from the literature what activity meets the criteria of being "sustainable." It might be claimed that sustainable *products or services* are needed. Or it might be claimed that the *industrial operations* of business organizations should be sustainable. Or it might be argued that sustainable *development initiatives* that utilize business products or services should be implemented. Ideally, it might be claimed that all three types of activity should be sustainable.

Second, most case studies used to demonstrate that BoP initiatives can be profitable have failed to demonstrate that the initiatives can also be environmentally sustainable. While such case studies may be forthcoming, the interpretation of their success at meeting the sustainability criteria will depend upon the particular conception of sustainability that is deployed. Third, the meaning of environmental sustainability, or sustainable development, has not been made clear by proponents of the BoP proposition. The concept of environmental sustainability applied to corporations, rather than to the development of nations in general, is incipient and underdeveloped. The idea is often associated with "eco-efficiency" or the idea that firms can conserve natural resources and save money in the process through increased efficiencies, new technologies, or alternative practices, but the idea of corporate environmental sustainability is considerably more complex than this (Banjeree 2008; Dyllick and Hockerts 2002; Goodland 1995). As we shall see below, TNC environmental practices impact the BoP in a variety of ways that need to be taken into account.

It is well understood that human population growth, and the economic growth that has facilitated increased human flourishing, are having a deleterious impact on the natural environment. Claims that BoP strategies should be sustainable are grounded in a shared understanding that the remarkable accomplishments of growth and development of the last century have been realized at significant environmental cost. To facilitate better understanding of the relationship between BoP ventures and environmental sustainability, it is necessary to clarify the ways in which TNCs and other business organizations can impact the natural environments in which BoP populations live.

The potential environmental impact of TNCs and other business enterprises on the BoP can usefully be divided into beneficial impacts that improve the natural environment in which the BoP live and harmful impacts that negatively affect the environment in ways that are deleterious to the health and welfare of BoP populations. Beneficial impacts on the local environment might include improved water, soil quality, or air quality, contributions to climate stability, or preservation of biodiversity. Harmful impacts on the local environment might include increased water pollution, air pollution, or soil pollution, climate instability, or deforestation. TNCs or other business enterprises that have no discernable impact or harm on the natural environment in which the BoP live may be said to have neutral environmental impact on BoP populations. In addition, the impact of TNCs and other firms on the BoP may be classified as directly harmful or indirectly harmful depending upon the causal chain of impact on BoP populations.

Direct Harm and Indirect Harm

Direct harm occurs when BoP products, services, or employment opportunities result in direct harm to BoP populations. For instance, Prahalad acknowledges that the single-serve packaging undertaken by Unilever and other companies produces excess packaging and will have negative environmental effects, but he also asserts that the "logic is obvious" for the use of small product units that would naturally use more packaging than larger units (2004, p. 41). He also dismisses recycling efforts as impractical (Prahalad 2004, p. 57). The disposal of non-compostable waste packing is ignored, as are the environmental impacts of chemicals contained in the shampoos and soaps on local ecosystems and groundwater. For example, the eutrophication of fresh water by phosphate-based detergents can result in a shortage of water for consumption. Alternative models such as selling biodegradable cleaning products in compostable packaging would be more sustainable.

The cement producer CEMEX provides affordable housing to BoP customers, but mining the limestone for cement results in deforestation and habitat loss and can negatively impact water tables, while the cement production process itself is estimated to produce 5% of total global carbon emissions contributing to climate change (Worrell et al. 2001). No discussion of carbon emissions offsets or biodiversity preservation is presented in relation to CEMEX's BoP strategy. The production and distribution of carbonated beverages targeted at the MEP, such as Coca-Cola products, draw from local water tables and produce carbon emissions while providing little or no nutritional value and contributing to tooth decay. Job creation is highlighted without consideration of the environmental and health impacts of increasing global distribution and consumption of sugary carbonated beverages. These cases demonstrate that business policies that aim to serve the BoP or the MEP in the interests of increased profitability may have adverse impacts in direct ways on those populations.

Indirectly harmful impacts occur when the general operations of TNCs or other business enterprises result in harmful externalities, such as air pollution or water pollution, that negatively impact BoP populations. It is well understood that "down wind" or "downstream" pollution disproportionately impacts poor populations given their inability to utilize market solutions to avoid pollution (Tietenberg and Lewis 2008). For example, industrial production of products targeting the MoP or the ToP can also result in the discharge or runoff of nitrates or phosphates leading to freshwater eutrophication. Toxic chemicals in airborne pollution can lead to birth defects, cancer, and respiratory illness.

Indirect harm to BoP populations also occurs when ecosystem services are altered or reduced via industrial activity. Ecosystems provide life-sustaining services, many of which cannot be replicated or substituted by human-made processes now or in the foreseeable future (Chivian and Bernstein 2008; Melillo and Sala 2008). These services include water and air purification, climate control, erosion control, the containment of animal diseases, flood mitigation, the binding and detoxification of pollutants in soils, sediments, and waters through vascular plants, fungi, and microorganisms, and climate stabilization through natural carbon sinks. Historically, critics argue, ecosystem services have been "grossly undervalued" by traditional economics (Goodland 1995, p. 7; see also Daly and Farley 2004). While the field of ecological economics has emerged to begin to address the value of ecosystem services and related problems at the intersections of economics and ecology, there has been little impact on business scholarship to date.

The regulating services provided by ecosystems are important to all humans, but they are especially important to the poor who are least able to adapt to environmental changes that adversely impact their welfare. Ecosystems are being degraded by industrial activity that is contributing to a loss of biodiversity and changes to Earth's climate (Chivian and Bernstein 2008; Meadows et al. 2004; IPCC 2007; IUCN 2011; Pimm et al. 2008; WWF 2010). For example, the Intergovernmental Panel of Climate Change (IPCC) has long reported that the major risks to human health from climate change include increases in malnutrition; increased deaths and illness due to heat waves, floods, storms, and droughts; more widespread diarrheal disease; increased cardio-respiratory disease due to higher concentrations of ozone; and increased infectious disease due to the expanded range of vectors (IPCC 2007).

The World Commission on Environment and Development (WCED) formally recognized the effect of environmental problems on populations of developing countries in the Brundtland Report (World Commission on Environment and Development 1987). The *Human Development Report* has discussed the connection of environmental concerns to social sustainability beginning with its 1994 report, and in its 1998 report recognized the "unfairness" of the fact that environmental degradation, including acid rain, ozone depletion, and climate change, causes the most suffering at the poorest socioeconomic levels, who are forced to adapt without the proper resources (UNDP 2010, p.18). The IPCC notes that climate change can be exacerbated by stresses such as poverty, inequitable resource sharing and access, food insecurity, economic globalization trends, political instability, conflict, and disease (IPCC 2007). These aggravators again bring the cycle back to the poor: the worst regional biodiversity losses are isolated to poorer regions, and impoverished countries cannot afford to readily find substitutes for lost resources such as water and farmable land (Meadows et al. 2004).

Links to Human Rights

One way of characterizing the harms caused by environmental degradation to persons living at the BoP is in terms of the deprivation of human rights. As has been argued in previous chapters, if any human rights can be defended, those rights include the rights to physical security (e.g., freedom from the harmful impacts of toxic pollution) and subsistence (e.g., unpolluted air and water). As we have seen in previous chapters, if one accepts the egalitarian principle that all humans are entitled to (at least) basic security and subsistence rights, then, absent arguments to the contrary, these rights will need to be taken into account. One way of taking these rights seriously is to ensure that they are protected via public policy. However, public policy is constrained by institutional failures and by government actions that contribute to environmental degradation. In a globalized economy that includes both developed and developing nations, notable disparities exist among nations in terms of resources, infrastructure, economic viability, political institutions, and regulatory frameworks. Nation-states create their environmental regulations, but these regulations are not enforced consistently as a result of incapacity, corruption, and other institutional factors. Corporations that operate within this environment often act as administrators of the rights of citizens in the absence of state-supported services and infrastructure (Matten and Crane 2005; Scherer et al. 2006). This observation is consistent with the tripartite framework, "Protect, Respect and Remedy," on business and human rights. BoP strategy advocates recognize this governance void and envision corporations—especially large, established, western TNCs—becoming able providers and enablers of rights in developing countries (Prahalad and Hart 2002).

The Paradox

The claim that strategic, profit-driven activities by business firms will greatly improve the welfare of those at the base of the pyramid is paradoxical because such economic activity often results in direct or indirect negative environmental impacts that will actually harm those at the base of the pyramid. The harm caused to those at the BoP by direct or indirect negative environmental impacts will be disproportionate relative to the harm caused to those at top of the pyramid (ToP) by virtue of the inability of those at the BoP to access resources necessary for adaptation. It should be emphasized that no conclusions follow from the mere identification of the paradox. For example, it does not follow from the identification of the paradox that profit-driven strategies aimed at the BoP ought not to be undertaken. Identifying the paradox does, however, facilitate a more complex analysis of the role of environmental sustainability in BoP market ventures.

TNC Impacts on the BoP

There are numerous combinations of ways in which TNCs can have positive and negative social and environmental impacts on the BoP. The nine possible combinations are indicated in Table 8.1. One way of characterizing the operative position of leading BoP venture proponents such as Prahalad and Hart is that profitable BoP ventures should be socially beneficial while having positive environmental impact (i) or neutral environmental impact (ii). However, as indicated in Table 8.1, there are numerous other possibilities regarding TNC social and environmental impacts in the BoP.

A BoP strategy with an exclusive focus on profitability can harm individuals at the BoP in two distinct ways. First, the product or service may undermine

Table 8.1 Potential Firm Impacts on the BoP

		TNC Social Impact	*TNC Environmental Impact*
BoP	1	+	+
	2	+	N
	3	+	−
	4	−	+
	5	−	−
	6	−	N
	7	N	+
	8	N	−
	9	N	N

Key: +, Positive; −, Negative; N, Neutral.

the ability of individuals at the BoP to improve their welfare. This might occur by means of providing goods or services that wrongly exploit individuals at the BoP by taking advantage of their vulnerability or desperation. In this state, they may be sold goods or services that are harmful or that inhibit their ability to improve life for themselves or their families. These include scenarios where TNCs, at least theoretically, have negative social impact but positive (iv) or neutral (vi) environmental impact, in addition to those scenarios in which they have both negative social and environmental impact (v). Second, the development of innovative products or services of benefit to the individuals at the BoP may harm these individuals by contributing over time to the degradation of the environment where they live, or to their capacity to make a living utilizing the natural resources of their local environment. These include scenarios where TNCs have positive (iii) or neutral (viii) social impact while having negative environmental impact. Both of these outcomes are consistent with a BoP strategy that is driven by a vision of BoP customers as a large, previously untapped consumer market.

Given the preceding analysis, there are two principal interpretations of the claim that BoP ventures should be environmentally sustainable. On the one hand, the claim can be read as a form of greenwashing in which the language of environmental sustainability is associated with a business strategy that has as its primary or exclusive aim the profitable exploitation of the world's poorest people, who, because of their poverty and lack of access to institutional resources (e.g., education, sanitation, and health care), are vulnerable and susceptible to harm. On this reading, invocations of environmental sustainability in BoP ventures aim to legitimize TNC activities that result in harmful externalities such as pollution and environmental degradation. This reading is consistent with the perspective of critical management scholars who regard corporate social responsibility claims as means of TNCs coopting stakeholders while avoiding responsibility for harmful activities such as negative environmental externalities (Banjeree 2003, 2008).

Alternatively, the claim that BoP ventures should be environmentally sustainable can be read as a call for genuinely innovative business strategies that implement products and services that reduce or eliminate harmful pollution and ecosystem degradation in BoP ventures while simultaneously supporting human capabilities and functioning and the attainment of basic human rights. On this interpretation, BoP ventures are not mere profit-seeking activities but more complexly motivated organizational ventures. Profit cannot be the sole motive informing BoP ventures if they are to have a beneficial impact on BoP populations. A more comprehensive strategy with a more complex set of motives is required if BoP populations are to benefit from new ventures that aim to take advantage of their collective spending power. Scholars, researchers, and managers should be clear about the multiple motives behind BoP ventures rather than reverting to the simplistic characterization of BoP ventures as mere profit seeking endeavors.

One often cited definition of environmentally, or ecologically, sustainable companies that is compatible with this reading of the BoP proposition is as follows:

> Ecologically sustainable companies use only natural resources that are consumed at a rate below the natural reproduction, or at a rate below the development of substitutes. They do not cause emissions that accumulate in the environment at a rate beyond the capacity of the natural system to absorb and assimilate these emissions. Finally they do not engage in activity that degrades eco-system services (Dyllick and Hockerts 2002, p. 133).

Such an account of environmental sustainability can accommodate both direct and indirect harm that TNCs may cause to BoP populations. While the definition sets a high bar for attaining sustainability, and while few firms may actually meet this definition of sustainability, the definition provides a more comprehensive basis for assessing TNC operations and their impact on the BoP.

Technological Innovation

Hart (2011) has defended one way that BoP strategies can have both positive social and positive environmental impacts. He describes "Green Sprout" technologies as those that are small-scale, distributed and highly innovative, developed locally and with labor-intensive resources. Hart emphasizes that these technologies are almost always notably disruptive in nature, especially to incumbent firms with large existing investments in technologies presently being employed. Green Sprout technologies are required to overcome barriers that may form due to this incumbency and thus are more well suited to underserved or otherwise untapped markets. Hart accordingly sees the BoP as an ideal market for these technologies to develop and grow. Examples of Green Sprout technologies include microturbines and small hydro electricity generation. The International Energy Agency notes that while the general success of most renewable energy sources explored within the past few decades has been tempered by an inability to reduce costs to levels competitive with conventional sources, small-scale renewable energy applications such as small hydro have been able to viably compete within the marketplace (2007, p. 6). Hart argues that, "Given their distributed character, when Green Sprout technologies 'scale,' they do so modularly, retaining their local focus, even as they expand to serve thousands or millions of communities around the world" (2011, p. 97). Essentially, Hart envisions applying the strengths—in innovation, technology, management, scale, and experience—of established corporations (which are mainly based in developed countries) on the open slate of the untapped BoP markets, which chiefly exist in developing countries. The resulting technologies and business models are then able to "trickle up" to markets at the ToP once they have become successful at the BoP (Hart 2011, p.85). However, a firm that might engage in such technological development may still have an indirectly harmful impact on the BoP via their industrial operations as we have shown above.

It is also true that for technical reasons, not all socially beneficial BoP products or services can follow the Green Sprout model. For example, CEMEX's Patrimonio Hoy program has clear social benefits to BoP customers, but cement production, even with the use of advanced energy efficient technology, has negative impacts on the BoP via carbon emissions and potentially via the loss of ecosystems and biodiversity. In cases such as this where BoP strategies have a positive social impact and a negative environmental impact, it may be possible to offset the negative environmental impact as an alternative. CEMEX has maintained an active biodiversity conservation program for many years and could undertake a comprehensive carbon offset initiative. The Cement Sustainability Initiative of the World Business Council for Sustainable Development, of which CEMEX is a member, might be used, for example, as a forum for articulating goals to offset biodiversity losses and for obtaining reliable data on the carbon dioxide emissions of cement and clinker plants, transportation fleets, and quarries, as well as data on the ecosystem impacts of quarries, so that carbon offsets tied to these negative impacts can be purchased.

A Pragmatic Solution via Business Policy

As we have seen, a theme present in much of the BoP literature is that profitably serving the BoP will improve the welfare of the billions of individuals at the BoP. The arguments of this chapter show that this is not necessarily the case. To help ensure that a BoP strategy consistently benefits BoP consumers, it should first be integrated into a broader business policy. Such a policy would integrate strategies aimed at the achievement of robust profitability with other values such as respect for basic human rights and environmental sustainability. A business policy should reflect the core values of an organization, which often reflect the values that its senior executives endorse, as well as basic norms of morality (Andrews 1971, p. 118; Elms et al. 2010). In this view, the pursuit of profit is constrained and informed by other values.

Our claim is not that an integrated BoP policy is a moral requirement and thereby should be adapted, for even if such a position could be persuasively defended, it would not by itself motivate many business leaders who did not share this conclusion. Nor do we claim that such a policy is instrumentally valuable insofar that it may improve relationships with NGOs, government bodies, and other stakeholders. This may be the case, and it may be a driver of some business policies, but we are not taking a position on this empirical question here (for discussion of these issues see, e.g. Orlitzky 2011; Vogel 2006). Our conclusion is that companies that target the BoP—in part because of organizational values such as respect for the basic rights of physical security and subsistence, or a more general commitment to empowerment of the poor, or to assuming a fair share of responsibility for enhancing human freedom through economic development—must incorporate environmental sustainability strategies into their broader business policies if they are to achieve the desired outcome of benefitting the BoP in profitable ways.

Table 8.2 illustrates the integrated business policy that is required to successfully incorporate a BoP strategy as an element of sustainable business policy. First, the impact of the goods or services on the BoP must be positive. Second, both direct and indirect environmental impact of the goods or services targeted at the BoP must be either neutral or positive. Third, the BoP initiative must be profitable. BoP strategists and corporate managers serving the BoP, in collaboration with BoP communities, must carefully evaluate BoP strategies to assess their social and environmental impact on BoP populations. Ideally, BoP strategies will have a positive social impact and a positive or neutral environmental impact.

Table 8.2 BoP Strategy as an Element of Sustainable Business Policy

	Firm Social Impact	*Firm Environmental Impact*	*Profitability*
BoP	+	N	+
	+	+	+

Key: +, Positive; N, Neutral.

An integrated business policy in which environmentally sustainable BoP strategies are embedded is necessary to achieve the goals initially conceived by BoP strategy proponents. We make no claims about the likelihood of the adaptation of such an integrated business policy, or the social, economic, or psychological factors that would facilitate the adaption of such a policy. Rather, we claim that the logic of the BoP proposition entails such an integrated business policy. Companies that target the BoP as customers, regardless of the underlying reasons, must incorporate environmental sustainability strategies into their broader business policies if they are to achieve the desired outcome of benefitting the BoP in profitable ways.

Conclusion

BoP strategies aim to benefit the poor and the TNCs serving them simultaneously. Our analysis shows that while such ventures remain a possibility, it is also true that profitable BoP ventures will not always result in socially beneficial activities or be the product of environmentally sustainable activities. If BoP ventures evolve in a similar way to historical economic growth patterns with only superficial concern for the environment, then these ventures will continue to undermine the natural environments in which BoP populations live and undermine social gains that may be realized by BoP ventures.

As has been argued above, the claim that profitable business activity will improve the welfare of those at the BoP is paradoxical because such activities often result in direct or indirect negative environmental impacts that will actually harm BoP populations, and it will do so in a manner disproportionate to those at higher tiers of the economic pyramid. Identification of this paradox does not undermine the core BoP proposition of doing well by doing good, but it does help to illustrate the need for more complex analyses of the role of environmental sustainability in BoP market ventures and in TNC operations. Advocates of BoP strategies tend to simplify the role of TNCs in alleviating poverty when they maintain that BoP ventures can be profitable, socially beneficial, and environmentally sustainable. To the extent that such an outcome is possible, the arguments of this chapter suggest that those outcomes will be the product of an integrated business policy that addresses not only the costs and benefits of products or services targeted at the BoP but overall firm impacts on the natural environments inhabited by BoP populations.

References

Academic Consortium on International Trade (2000). Letter to University Presidents (29 July). http://www.fordschool.umich.edu/rsie/acit/Documents/Anti-Sweatshop LetterPage.html.

Altman, D.G., Rego, L., and Ross, P. (2009). Expanding opportunity at the base of the pyramid. *People & Strategy* 32 (2): 46–51.

Alwang, J., Siegel, P., and Jorgensen, S. (2001). *Vulnerability: A View from Different Disciplines*, World Bank Discussion Paper No. 0115. Washington, DC: World Bank Group.

Anderson, E. (1995). *Values in Ethics and Economics*. Cambridge, MA: Harvard University Press.

Anderson, J.L. and Markides, C. (2007). Strategic innovation at the base of the pyramid. *MIT Sloan Management Review* 49 (1): 83–88.

Anderson, J.L., Markides, C., and Kupp, M. (2010). The last frontier: market creation in conflict zones, deep rural areas, and urban slums. *California Management Review* 52 (4): 6–28.

Andrews, K.R. (ed.) (1971). *The Concept of Corporate Strategy*, 2e. 1980; 3rd ed. 1987. Homewood, IL: Irwin.

Armstrong, J.S. (1977). Social irresponsibility in management. *Journal of Business Research* 5: 185–213.

Arneson, R.J. (1981). What's wrong with exploitation? *Ethics* 91: 202–227.

Arnold, D.G. (2003a). Exploitation and the sweatshop quandary. *Business Ethics Quarterly* 13 (2): 243–256.

Arnold, D.G. (2003b). Libertarian theories of the corporation and global capitalism. *Journal of Business Ethics* 48 (2003): 155–173.

Arnold, D.G. (2006). Corporate moral agency. *Midwest Studies in Philosophy, Volume XXX: "Shared Intentions and Collective Responsibility"* (2006) 30: 279–291.

The Ethics of Global Business, First Edition. Denis G. Arnold.
© 2023 John Wiley & Sons Ltd. Published 2023 by John Wiley & Sons Ltd.

Arnold, D.G. (2009). Working conditions: Safety and sweatshops. In: *The Oxford Handbook of Business Ethics* (ed. G. Brenkert and T. Beauchamp), 628–656. Oxford University Press.

Arnold, D.G. (2010). Transnational corporations and the duty to respect basic human rights. *Business Ethics Quarterly* 20 (3): 371–399.

Arnold, D.G. (2013). Global justice and international business. *Business Ethics Quarterly* 23 (1): 125–143.

Arnold, D.G. and Bowie, N.E. (2003). Sweatshops and respect for persons. *Business Ethics Quarterly* 13 (2): 221–242.

Arnold, D.G. and Bowie, N.E. (2007). Respect for workers in global supply chains: advancing the debate over sweatshops. *Business Ethics Quarterly* 17 (1): 135–145.

Arnold, D.G. and Hartman, L.P. (Winter 2003). Moral imagination and the future of sweatshops. *Business and Society Review* 108 (4): 425–461.

Arnold, D.G. and Hartman, L.P. (2005). Beyond sweatshops: positive deviancy and global labor practices. *Business Ethics: A European Review* 14 (3): 206–222.

Arnold, D.G. and Hartman, L. (2006). Worker rights and low wage industrialization: how to avoid sweatshops. *Human Rights Quarterly* 28 (3): 676–700.

Arnold, D.G. and Williams, L.H.D. (2012). The paradox at the base of the pyramid: environmental sustainability and market-based poverty alleviation. *International Journal of Technology Management* 60 (1/2): 44–59.

Banerjee, S.B. (2010). Governing the global corporation: a critical perspective. *Business Ethics Quarterly* 20 (2): 265–274.

Banerjee, A.V. and Duflo, E. (2007). The economic lives of the poor. *Journal of Economic Perspectives* 21 (1): 141–167.

Banerjee, A.V. and Duflo, E. (2011). *Poor Economics: A Radical Rethinking of the Way to Fight Global Poverty*. Public Affairs.

Banjeree, S.B. (2003). Who sustains whose development? Sustainable development and the reinvention of nature. *Organization Studies* 24 (1): 143–180.

Banjeree, S.B. (2008). Corporate social responsibility: the good, the bad, and the ugly. *Critical Sociology* 34 (1): 51–79.

Barki, E. and Parente, J. (2010). Consumer behaviour of the base of the pyramid market in Brazil. *Greener Management International* 56: 11–23.

Barstow, D. (2012). Vast Mexico bribery case hushed up by Wal-Mart after top-level struggle. *The New York Times* (22 April), p. A1.

Barstow, D. and von Bertrab, A.X. (2012). The Bribery Aisle: how Wal-Mart got its way in Mexico. *The New York Times* (18 December), p. A1.

Bartlett, C.A. and Ghoshal, S. (2002). *Managing Across Borders: The Transnational Solution*, 2e. Harvard Business School Press.

Beitz, C. (1979). *Political Theory and International Relations*. Princeton, NJ: Princeton University Press.

Besson, S. (2015). The bearers of human rights duties and responsibilities for human rights: a quiet (R) evolution. *Social Philosophy and Policy* 32 (1): 254.

Bhagwati, J. (2004). *In Defense of Globalization*. New York: Oxford University Press.

Bishop, J.D. (2012). The limits of corporate human rights obligations and the rights of for-profit corporations. *Business Ethics Quarterly* 22 (1): 119–144.

Blake, M. (2012). Global distributive justice: why political philosophy needs political science. *Annual Review of Political Science* 15: 121–136.

Boal, W.M. and Ransom, M.R. (1997). Monopsony in the labor market. *Journal of Economic Literature* 35: 86–112.

Bratman, M. (1987). *Intention, Plans, and Practical Reason*. Cambridge: Harvard University Press.

Bratman, M. (1999). *Faces of Intention: Selected Essays on Intention and Agency*. Cambridge: Harvard University Press.

Brenkert, G.G. (1998). Marketing and the vulnerable. *Business Ethics Quarterly*, The Ruffin Series 1: 7–20.

Brock, G. (2009). *Global Justice: A Cosmopolitan Account*. Oxford: Oxford University Press.

Buchanan, A. (2000). Rawls's law of peoples: rules for a vanished Westphalian world. *Ethics* 110 (4): 697–721.

Buchanan, A.E. (2013). *The Heart of Human Rights*. New York: Oxford University Press.

Buchanan, A. and Keohane, R.O. (2006). The legitimacy of global governance institutions. *Ethics & International Affairs* 20 (4): 405–437.

Business Call to Action (2008). The Coca-Cola Company: Enabling jobs and opportunity. http://www.businesscalltoaction.org/wp-content/files_mf/1286826974CocaColaCaseStudyFORWeb.pdf (accessed 12 January 2013).

Business Leaders Initiative on Human Rights (2009). Policy Report 4. http://www.blihr.org/ (accessed 12 January 2013.).

Business Week/Harris Poll (2000). How business rates: by the numbers. http://www.businessweek.com/2000/00_37/b3698004.htm (accessed 23 November 2015).

Campbell, T. (2006). A human rights approach to developing voluntary codes of conduct for multinational corporations. *Business Ethics Quarterly* 16 (2): 255–269.

Caney, S. (2005). *Justice Beyond Borders: A Global Political Theory*. Oxford: Oxford University Press.

Caney, S. (2009). Climate change, human rights and moral thresholds. In: *Human Rights and Climate Change* (ed. S. Humphreys). Cambridge University Press.

Casson, M. (1982). *The Entrepreneur*. Barnes & Noble Books.

Central Intelligence Agency (2011). World fact book, "literacy." https://www.cia.gov/library/publications/the-world-factbook/fields/2103.html (accessed 12 January 2013.).

Chakravarti, D. (2006). Voices unheard: the psychology of consumption in poverty and development. *Journal of Consumer Psychology* 16 (4): 363–376.

Chan, J. (1999). A Confucian perspective on human rights for contemporary China. In: *The East Asian Challenge for Human Rights* (ed. J.R. Bauer and D.A. Bell), 212–237. Cambridge: Cambridge University Press.

Chavez, A., Martinez, C., and Soberanes, B. (1995). The effect of malnutrition on human development: a 24-year study of well-nourished and malnourished children living in a poor Mexican village. In: *Community-Based Longitudinal Nutrition* and Health Studies: Classic Examples from Guatemala, Haiti, and Mexico* (ed. N.S. Scrimshaw), 79–124. Boston: International Nutrition Foundation for Developing Countries.

Chivian, E. and Bernstein, A. (2008). How is biodiversity threatened by human activity? In: *Sustaining Life: How Human Health Depends on Biodiversity* (ed. E. In Chivian and A. Bernstein), 29–73. Oxford University Press.

Ci, J. (2005). Taking the reasons for human rights seriously. *Political Theory* 33 (2): 243–265.

Clapham, A. (1993). *Human Rights in the Private Sphere*, 138. Oxford: Clarendon Press.

Cohen, G.A. (1987). Are disadvantaged workers who take hazardous jobs forced to take hazardous jobs? In: *Moral Rights in the Workplace* (ed. G. Ezorsky). Albany: State University of New York Press.

Cohen, J. and Sabin, C. (2006). Global democracy? *New York University Journal of International Law and Politics* 37 (4): 763–797.

Collins, D., Morduch, J., Rutherford, S., and Ruthven, O. (2009). *Portfolios of the Poor: How the World's Poor Live on $2 a Day*. Princeton University Press.

Conner, T. (2002). *We Are Not Machines: Indonesian Nike and Adidas Workers*, 1–36. The Clean Clothes Campaign, Global Exchange, Maquila Solidarity Network, Oxfam Canada, and Oxfam Community Abroad.

Cragg, W. (2002). Human rights and business ethics: Fashioning a new social contract. *The Journal of Business Ethics* 27: 205–214.

Cragg, W. (2004). Human rights, globalisation and the modern shareholder owned corporation. In: *Human Rights and the Moral Responsibilities of Corporate and Public Sector Organisations* (ed. T. Campbell and S. Miller). Kluwer Academic Publishers.

Cragg, W. (2009). Business and human rights: a principle and value based analysis. In: *The Oxford Handbook of Business Ethics* (ed. G. Brenkert and T. Beauchamp). New York: Oxford University Press.

Cragg, W. (2012). Ethics, enlightened self interest and the corporate responsibility to respect human rights: a critical look at the justificatory foundations of the proposed UN human rights framework. *Business Ethics Quarterly* 22 (1): 9–36.

Cragg, W., Arnold, D.G., and Muchlinski, P. (2012). Human rights and business. *Business Ethics Quarterly* 22 (1): 1–7.

Daly, H.E. and Farley, J. (2004). *Ecological Economics: Principles and Applications*. Island Press.

DeRose, L., Messer, E., and Millman, S. (1998). *Who's Hungry? And How Do We Know? Food Shortage, Poverty, and Deprivation*. United Nations University Press.

Deva, S. (2008). Global compact: a critique of the U.N.'s "Public-Private" partnership for promoting corporate citizenship. *Syracuse Journal of International Law and Commerce* 34: 107–151.

Doh, J.B.W., Husted, D.M., and Santoro, M. (2010). Ahoy there! toward greater congruence and synergy between international business and business ethics theory and research. *Business Ethics Quarterly* 20 (3): 481–502.

Donaldson, T. (1991). *The Ethics of International Business*. Oxford: Oxford University Press.

Donaldson, T. and Dunfee, T.W. (1999). *Ties That Bind: A Social Contracts Approach to Business Ethics*. Boston: Harvard Business School Press.

Donnelly, J. (1999). Human rights, democracy, and development. *Human Rights Quarterly* 21 (3): 608–632.

Donnelly, J. (2003). In defense of the universal declaration model. In: *International Human Rights in the 21st Century: Protecting the Rights of Groups* (ed. G.M. Lyons and J. Mayall), 20–48. Boston: Rowman & Littlefield Publisher.

Dunning, J. (2001). *Global Capitalism at Bay?* Routledge.

Dworkin, G. (1988). *The Theory and Practice of Autonomy*. Cambridge: Cambridge University Press.

Dyllick, T. and Hockerts, K. (2002). Beyond the business case for corporate sustainability. *Business Strategy and the Environment* 11: 130–141.

Elms, H.S., Brammer, J.D., Harris, R.A., and Phillips (2010). New directions in strategic management and business ethics. *Business Ethics Quarterly* 20 (3): 401–425.

Elster, J. (1989). *Nuts and Bolts for the Social Sciences*. Cambridge: Cambridge University Press.

Epstein, E.M. (1969). *The Corporation in American Politics*. Englewood Cliffs: Prentice Hall.

Ernst and Young (1997). Environmental and Labor Practices Audit of the Tae Kwang Vina Industrial Ltd. Co., Vietnam (13 January 1997).

European Commission (2011). A renewed EU strategy 2011-14 for Corporate Social Responsibility. Communication From the Commission to the European Parliament, the Council, the European Economic and Social Committee and the Committee of the Regions, Com 681.

Faden, R. and Beauchamp, T.L. (2009). The right to risk information and the right to refuse workplace hazards. In: *Ethical Theory and Business*, 8e (ed. T.L. Beauchamp, N.E. Bowie and D.G. Arnold), 129–136. Englewood Cliffs, NJ: Pearson Prentice-Hall.

Fauver, L. and Fuerst, M.E. (2006). Does good corporate governance include employee representation? Evidence from German corporate boards. *Journal of Financial Economics* 82 (3): 673–710.

Feinberg, J. (1973). *Social Philosophy*. Englewood Cliffs: Prentice Hall.

Fitch, B. and Sorensen, L. (2007). The case for accelerating profit-making at the base of the pyramid: What could and should the donor community be seeking to do, and what results should it expect? *Journal of International Development* 19 (6): 781–792.

Frankfurt, H.G. (1988). *The Importance of What We Care About*. Cambridge: Cambridge University Press.

Freedom House (2020). Freedom in the Word. https://freedomhouse.org/report/freedom-world.

French, P.A. (1979). The corporation as a moral person. *American Philosophical Quarterly* 16 (3): 207–215.

French, P. (1996). Integrity, intentions, and corporations. *American Business Law Journal* 34: 141–155.

Friedman, M. (1970). The social responsibility of business is to increase its profits. *The New York Times Magazine* (13 September).

Gardetti, M.A. and D'Andrea, G. (2010). Masisa Argentina and the evolution of its strategy at the base of the pyramid: an alternative to the BoP protocol process? *Greener Management International* 56: 75–91.

George, D. and Richard, T. (1993). *Competing with Integrity in International Business.* New York: Oxford University Press.

Ghoshal, S. (2005). Bad management theories are destroying good management practices. *Academy of Management Learning & Education* 4 (1): 75–91.

Gond, J., Palazzo, G., and Basu, K. (2009). Reconsidering instrumental corporate social responsibility through the mafia metaphor. *Business Ethics Quarterly* 19 (1): 57–85.

Goodland, R. (1995). The concept of environmental sustainability. *Annual Review of Ecology and Systematics* 26 (1): 1–24.

Gordon, N. (2007). Oral health care for children attending a malnutrition clinic in South Africa. *International Journal of Dental Hygiene* 5 (3): 180–186.

Griffin, J. (2008). *On Human Rights.* Oxford University Press.

Hall, P.A. and Soskice, D. (ed.) (2001). *Varieties of Capitalism: The Institutional Foundations of Comparative Advantage.* Oxford University Press.

Hamel, G. and Prahalad, C.K. (1989). Strategic intent. *Harvard Business Review* 67 (3): 148–161.

Hammond, A.L., Kramer, W.J., Katz, R.S. et al. (2007). *The Next 4 Billion: Market Size and Business Strategy at the Base of the Pyramid.* Washington, DC: World Resources Institute and International Finance Corporation.

Hanson, M. and Powell, K. (2006). Procter and Gamble pur purifier of waterTM (A): developing the product and taking it to market. INSEAD.

Hart, H.L.A. (1955). Are there any natural rights? *The Philosophical Review* 64 (2): 175–191.

Hart, S.L. (2011). Taking the green leap to the base of the pyramid. In: *Next Generation Business Strategies for the Base of the Pyramid: New Approaches for Building Mutual Value* (ed. T. London and S.L. Hart), 79–102. Pearson Education.

Hart Research Associates (2010). Protecting Democracy From Unlimited Corporate Spending, Results from a National Survey among 1000 Voters on the Citizens United Decision Conducted June 6–7, 2010. http://www.pfaw.org/sites/default/files/CitUPoll-PFAW.pdf.

Hawarden, V. and Barnard, E. (2011). *Danimal in South Africa: Management Innovation at the Bottom of the Pyramid.* Ivey Publishing.

Held, D. (2002). Globalization, corporate practice and cosmopolitan social standards. *Contemporary Political Theory* 1 (1): 59–78.

Heller, K.E., Burt, B.A., and Eklund, S.A. (2001). Sugared soda consumption and dental caries in the United States. *Journal of Dental Research* 80 (10): 1949–1953.

Henderson, D. (2001). *Misguided Virtue: False Notions of Corporate Social Responsibility*. London: Institute of Economic Affairs.

Herman, B. (1993). *The Practice of Moral Judgment*. Harvard University Press.

Hsieh, N. (2004). The obligations of transnational corporations: rawlsian justice and the duty of assistance. *Business Ethics Quarterly* 14 (4): 643–661.

Hsieh, N. (2009). Does global business have a responsibility to promote just institutions? *Business Ethics Quarterly* 19 (2): 251–273.

Hsieh, N. (2015). Should business have human rights obligations? *Journal of Human Rights* 14 (2): 218–236, 219.

Hsieh, N. (2017). Business responsibilities for human rights. *Business and Human Rights Journal* 2 (2): 297–309.

Human Rights Council (2008). Protect, Respect and Remedy: A Framework for Business and Human Rights. A/HRC/8/5 17 (7 April 2008).

Human Rights Council (2011). Guiding Principles on Business and Human Rights: Implementing the United Nations 'Protect, Respect and Remedy' Framework. A/HRC/17/31 (21 March 2011) 13.

Human Rights Watch (1998). A Job or Your Rights: Continued Sex Discrimination in Mexico's Maquiladora Sector, Volume 10, No. 1(B) December 1998. http://www.hrw.org/reports98/women2/ (accessed 15 December 2021).

Human Rights Watch (2011). *You'll Be Fired If You Refuse: Labor Abuses in Zambia's Chinese State-owned Copper Mines*. Human Rights Watch (3 November 2011).

Ignatieff, M. (2001). Human rights as idolatry. In: *Human Rights as Politics and Idolatry* (ed. A. Gutman). Princeton, NJ: Princeton University Press.

Intergovernmental Panel on Climate Change (2007). Summary for policymakers. In: *Climate Change 2007: Impacts, Adaptation and Vulnerability. Contribution of Working Group II to the Fourth Assessment Report of the Intergovernmental Panel on Climate Change* (ed. M.L. Parry, O.F. Canziani, J.P. Palutikof, et al.). Cambridge University Press.

International Chamber of Commerce and the International Organisation of Employers (2003). Joint views of ICC and the IOE on the draft "Norms on the Responsibilities of Transnational Corporations and Other Business Enterprises with regard to Human Rights. 24 November 2003.

International Energy Agency (2007). *Renewables in Global Energy Supply: An IEA Fact Sheet*. OECD/IEA http://www.iea.org/papers/2006/renewable_factsheet.pdf.

International Labour Office (2010). *International Labour Migration: A Rights-Based Approach*. Geneva: International Labour Office.

International Labour Organization (1999). *Decent Work: Report of the Director General*. Geneva: International Labour Office.

Ireland, J. (2008). Lessons for successful BOP marketing from Caracas' slums. *Journal of Consumer Marketing* 25 (7): 430–438.

ITC e-Choupal (2011). ITC website: e-Choupal: Let's Put India First. http://www.itcportal.com/sustainability/lets-put-india-first/echoupal.aspx.

IUCN (2011). About the IUCN red list, 24 May 2011. http://www.iucn.org/about/work/programmes/species/red_list/about_the_red_list/.

Jones, T.M. and Felps, W. (2013). Shareholder wealth maximization and social welfare: a utilitarian critique. *Business Ethics Quarterly 23* (2): 207–238.

Joseph, S. (2004). *Corporations and Transnational Human Rights Litigation*, vol. 4. Hart Publishing.

Kane, R. (1998). *The Significance of Free Will*. Oxford: Oxford University Press.

Kant, I. (1990). *Foundations of the Metaphysics of Morals*. trans. L. W. Beck. Macmillan.

Kaplinsky, R., Robinson, S., and Willenbockel, D. (2007). *Asian Drivers and Sub-Saharan Africa – The Challenge to Development Strategy*, vol. 4. Rockefeller Foundation.

Karnani, A. (2007). The mirage of marketing to the bottom of the pyramid: how the private sector can help alleviate poverty. *California Management Review 49* (4): 90–111.

Keohane, R.O. (2011). Global governance legitimacy. *Review of International Political Economy 18* (1): 99–109.

Knight, P. (1998). New Labor Initiatives. Speech delivered to the National Press Club, Washington, DC (12 May).

Kobrin, S.J. (2009). Private political authority and public responsibility: transnational politics, transnational firms, and human rights. *Business Ethics Quarterly 19* (3): 349–374.

Kotler, P., Roberto, N., and Leisner, T. (2006). Alleviating poverty: a macro/micro marketing perspective. *Journal of Macromarketing 26* (2): 233–239.

Kristof, N.D. (2000). Brutal drive. In: *Thunder From the East: Portrait of a Rising Asia* (ed. N.D. Kristof and S. WuDunn). New York: Alfred A. Knopf.

Krugman, P. (1999). *In Praise of Cheap Labor: Bad Jobs at Bad Wages Are Better Than No Wages at All*. in his *The Accidental Theorist and Other Dispatches from the Dismal Science*. New York: W.W. Norton.

Landrum, N.E. (2007). Advancing the base of the pyramid debate. *Strategic Management Review 1* (1): 1–12.

Levis, J. (2006). Adoption of corporate social responsibility codes by multinational companies. *Journal of Asian Economics 17* (1): 50–55.

Lindblom, C.E. (1977). *Politics and Markets: The World's Political-Economic Systems*. New York: Basic Books.

Liu, Y., Rao, K., Hu, T.-W. et al. (2006). Cigarette smoking and poverty in China. *Social Science and Medicine 63*: 2784–2790.

Lomasky, L.E. (1987). *Persons, Rights, and the Moral Community*. Oxford University Press.

London, T. and Hart, S.L. (2004). Reinventing strategies for emerging markets: beyond the transnational model. *Journal of International Business Studies 35* (5): 350–370.

London, T. and Hart, S.L. (2011). *Next Generation Business Strategies for the Base of the Pyramid: New Approaches for Building Mutual Value*. Pearson Education, Inc.

Lux, S., Crook, T.R., and Woehr, D.J. (2011). Mixing business with politics: a meta-analysis of the antecedents and outcomes of corporate political activity. *Journal of Management 37* (1): 223–247.

Macarov, D. (2003). *What the Market Does to People: Privatization, Globalization, and Poverty*. Clarity Press.

Machan, T. (1987). Rights and myths in the workplace. In: *Moral Rights in the Workplace* (ed. G. Ezorsky). Albany: State University of New York Press.

Maitland, I. (2009). The great non-debate over international sweatshops. Reprinted in. In: *Ethical Theory and Business*, 9e (ed. T.L. Beauchamp, N.E. Bowie and D.G. Arnold), 597–607. Upper Saddle River, NJ: Pearson Prentice-Hall [first published in *British Academy of Management Conference Proceedings* 240–265 (1997)].

Makinen, J. and Kourula, A. (2012). Pluralism in political corporate responsibility. *Business Ethics Quarterly* 22 (4): 649–678.

Malaviya, P., Singhal, A., and Svenkerud, J.P. (2004). Telenor in Bangladesh (C): The way forward. INSEAD.

Matten, D. and Crane, A. (2005). Corporate citizenship: toward an extended theoretical conceptualization. *Academy of Management Review* 30 (1): 169–179.

McMullen, J.S. and Shepherd, D.A. (2006). Entrepreneurial action and the role of uncertainty in the theory of the entrepreneur. *Academy of Management Review* 31 (1): 132–152.

McWilliams, A. and Siegel, D. (2001). Corporate social responsibility: a theory of the firm perspective. *Academy of Management Review* 26 (1): 117–127.

McWilliams, A., Siegel, D.S., and Wright, P.M. (2006). Corporate social responsibility: Strategic implications. *Journal of management studies* 43 (1): 1–18.

Meadows, D.H., Randers, J., and Meadows, D. (2004). *Limits to Growth: The 30-Year Update*. Chelsea Green.

Melden, A.I. (1977). *Rights and Persons*. University of California Press.

Melillo, J. and Sala, O. (2008). Ecosystem services. In: *Sustaining Life: How Human Health Depends on Biodiversity* (ed. E. Chivian and A. Bernstein), 75–115. Oxford University Press.

Meyer, K.E., Mudambi, R., and Narula, R. (2011). Multinational enterprises and local contexts: the opportunities and challenges of multiple embeddedness. *Journal of Management Studies* 48: 235–252.

Michaelson, C. (2010). Revisiting the global business ethics question. *Business Ethics Quarterly* 20 (2): 237–251.

Mitchell, N.J. (1997). *The Conspicuous Corporation: Business, Public Policy, and Representative Democracy*. Ann Arbor: University of Michigan Press.

Muchlinski, P.T. (2001). Human rights and multinationals: is there a problem. *International Affairs* 77 (1): 31–47.

Muchlinski, P.T. (2007). *Multinational Enterprises and the Law*. Oxford University Press.

Murphy, L.B. (1998). Institutions and the demands of justice. *Philosophy & Public Affairs* 27 (4): 251–294.

Nagel, T. (1991). *Equality and partiality*. Oxford University Press.

Nagel, T. (1995). Personal rights and public space. *Philosophy & Public Affairs* 24 (2): 83–107.

Nagel, T. (2005). The problem of global justice. *Philosophy & Public Affairs* 33 (2): 113–147.

Narayan, D., Chambers, R., Shah, M.K., and Petesch, P. (2000). *Voices of the Poor: Crying Out for Change*. Oxford University Press.

National Labor Committee (1995). *The U.S. in Haiti: How to Get Rich on 11 Cents an Hour*.

Nelson, K. and Ware, R. (ed.) (1997). *Exploitation*. Atlantic Highlands, NJ: Humanities Press.

Nickel, J. (2009). Human rights. In: *The Stanford Encyclopedia of Philosophy (Spring 2009 Edition)* (ed. E.N. Zalta). Stanford University http://plato.stanford.edu/archives/spr2009/entries/rights-human/.

Norberg, J. (2003). *In Defense of Global Capitalism*. Washington, DC: Cato Institute.

Nozick, R. (1974). *Anarchy, State, and Utopia*. New York: Basic Books.

Nussbaum, M. (2007). Human rights and capabilities. *Harvard Human Rights Journal* 20: 21–24.

O'Neill, O. (1996). *Towards Justice and Virtue: A Constructive Account of Practical Reasoning*. Cambridge University Press.

O'Neill, O. (2000). *Bounds of Justice*. Cambridge University Press.

O'Neill, O. (2001). Agents of justice. In: *Global Justice* (ed. T. Pogge). Blackwell.

O'Neill, O. (2005). The dark side of human rights. *International Affairs* 81 (2): 427–439.

Orlitzky, M. (2011). Institutional logics in the study of organizations: the social construction of the relationship between corporate social and financial performance. *Business Ethics Quarterly* 21 (3): 409–444.

Orts, E.W. (2013). *Business Persons: A Legal Theory of the Firm*. Oxford University Press.

Palazzo, G. and Scherer, A.G. (2006). Corporate legitimacy as deliberation. A communicative framework. *Journal of Business Ethics* 61 (1): 71–88.

Pettit, P. (1992). Institutions. In: *Encyclopedia of Ethics* (ed. L.C. Becker and C.B. Becker). Garland Publishing.

Pimm, S.L., Alves, M.A.S., Chivian, E., and Bernstein, A. (2008). What is biodiversity? In: *Sustaining Life: How Human Health Depends on Biodiversity* (ed. E. Chivian and A. Bernstein), 3–27. Oxford University Press.

Pogge, T. (2002a). Human rights and human responsibilities. In: *Global Justice and Transnational Politics* (ed. P. De Greiff and C. Cronin). MIT Press.

Pogge, T. (2002b). *World Poverty and Human Rights*. Polity Press.

Pogge, T. (2005). Real world justice. *The Journal of Ethics* 9 (1–2): 29–53.

Poll, H. (2012). PACs, Big Companies, Lobbyists, and Banks and Financial Institutions Seen by Strong Majorities as Having Too Much Power and Influence in DC, May 29. https://theharrispoll.com/new-york-n-y-may-29-2012-when-one-thinks-about-how-washington-d-c-works-certain-groups-are-always-seen-as-being-too-powerful-and-wielding-too-much-influence-whether-in-the-halls-of-congress/.

Pollin, R., Burns, J., and Heintz, J. (2004). Global apparel production and sweatshop labour: can raising retails prices finance living wages? *Cambridge Journal of Economics* 28 (2): 153–171.

Powell, B. (2006). In reply to sweatshop sophistries. *Human Rights Quarterly* 28: 1032–1042.

Prahalad, C.K. (2004). *The Fortune at the Bottom of the Pyramid: Eradicating Poverty Through Profits*. Wharton School Publishing.

Prahalad, C.K. and Hammond, A. (2002). Serving the world's poor, profitably. *Harvard Business Review* 80 (9): 48–57.

Prahalad, C.K. and Hart, S.L. (2002). The fortune at the bottom of the pyramid. *Strategy+Business* 26: 2–14.

Prakash Sethi, S. (1999). Codes of conduct for multinational corporations: an idea whose time has come. *Business and Society Review* 104 (3): 225–241.

Prakash Sethi, S. (2003). *Setting Global Standards: Guidelines for Creating Codes of Conduct in Multinational Corporations*. Hoboken, NJ: Wiley.

Rajendrah, A. and Shah, T. (2003). *Annapurna Salt: Public Health and Private Enterprise*. University of Michigan Business School.

Rawls, J. (1955). Two concepts of rules. *The Philosophical Review* 64: 3–32.

Rawls, J. (1971). *A Theory of Justice*. Cambridge, MA: Harvard University Press.

Rawls, J. (1996). *Political Liberalism*. Columbia University Press.

Rawls, J. (1999). *Law of Peoples*. Harvard University Press.

Raz, J. (2001). *Value, Respect, and Attachment*. Cambridge: Cambridge University Press.

Reitberger, M. (2008). Poverty, negative duties, and the global institutional order. *Politics, Philosophy & Economics* 7 (4): 379–402.

Rodman, K.A. (1998). "Think globally, punish locally": nonstate actors, multinational corporations, and human rights sanctions. *Ethics & International Affairs* 12 (1): 19–41.

Roemer, J. (1982). *A General Theory of Exploitation and Class*. Cambridge, MA: Harvard University Press.

Rorty, R. (1993). Human rights, rationality and sentimentality. In: *On Human Rights* (ed. S. Shute and S. Hurley). New York: Basic Books.

Ruggie, J.G. (2008). *Protect, Respect and Remedy: A Framework for Business and Human Rights*. (Doc A/HRC/8/5). Washington, DC: United Nations.

Rugman, A.M. and Doh, J.P. (2008). *Multinationals and Development*. New Haven, CT: Yale University Press.

Sachs, J.D. (2005). *The End of Poverty*. New York: The Penguin Press.

Santoro, M.A. (2000). *Profits and Principles: Global Capitalism and Human Rights in China*. Cornell University Press.

Santoro, M.A. (2010). Post-westphalia and its discontents. *Business Ethics Quarterly* 20 (2): 285–297.

Santos, N.J.C. and Laczniak, G.R. (2009). Marketing to the poor: An integrative justice model for engaging impoverished market segments. *Journal of Public Policy & Marketing* 28 (1): 3–15.

Sceats, S. and Breslin, S. (2012). *China and the International Human Rights System*. Chatham House, The Royal Institute of International Affairs.

Schaefer, B. (2005). Human rights: problems with the foundationless approach. *Social Theory and Practice* 31 (1): 1–24, 6.

Scheffler, S. (2001). *Boudaries and Allegiances: Problems of Justice and Responsibility in Liberal Thought*. Oxford University Press.

Scherer, A.G. and Palazzo, G. (2007). Toward a political conception of corporate responsibility: Business and society seen from a Habermasian perspective. *Academy of Management Review* 32 (4): 1096–1120.

Scherer, A.G. and Palazzo, G. (2011). The new political role of business in a globalized world: a review of a new perspective on CSR and its implications for the firm, governance, and democracy. *Journal of Management Studies* 48 (4): 899–931.

Scherer, A.G., Palazzo, G., and Baumann, D. (2006). Global rules and private actors: toward a new role of the transnational corporation in global governance. *Business Ethics Quarterly* 16 (4): 505–532.

Schwartz, J. (1995). In defence of exploitation. *Economics and Philosophy* 11: 275–307.

Seelos, C. and Mair, J. (2007). Profitable business models and market creation in the context of deep poverty: A strategic view. *Academy of Management Perspectives* 21 (4): 49–63.

Sen, A.K. (1990). Individual freedom as social commitment. *India International Centre Quarterly* 17 (1): 101–115.

Sen, A.K. (1993). Capability and well-being. In: *The Quality of Life* (ed. M.C. Nussbaum and A.K. Sen), 30–53. Clarendon Press.

Sen, A.K. (1999). *Development as Freedom*. Oxford University Press.

Sen, A. (2000). East and west: the reach of reason. *New York Review of Books* 47 (12): 33–38.

Sen, A. (2004). Elements of a theory of human rights. *Philosophy and Public Affairs* (Fall 2004) 32 (4): 315–356.

Sen, A.K. (2005). Human rights and capabilities. *Journal of Human Development* 6 (2): 151–156.

Sen, A.K. (2009). *The Idea of Justice*. Massachusetts: Belknap Press.

Shane, S. and Venkataraman, S. (2000). The promise of entrepreneurship as a field of research. *Academy of Management Review* 25 (1): 217–226.

Shankleman, J. (2009). *Going Global: Chinese Oil and Mining Companies and the Governance of Resource Wealth*. Washington, DC: Woodrow Wilson International Center for Scholars.

Shelton, G. and Kabemba, C. (2012). *Winwin Partnership? China, Southern Africa and the Extractive Industries*. Johannesburg: Southern Africa Resource Watch.

Shue, H. (1988). Mediating duties. *Ethics* 98 (1988): 687–704.

Shue, H. (1996). *Basic Rights: Subsistence, Affluence, and U.S. Foreign Policy*, revised e. Princeton University Press.

Shukla, S. and Bairiganjan, S. (2011). *The Base of the Pyramid Distribution Challenge: Evaluating Alternate Distribution Models of Energy Products for Rural Base of Pyramid India*. Centre for Development Finance, Institute for Financial and Management Research.

Singer, P. (1972). Famine, affluence and morality. *Philosophy and Public Affairs* 1 (3): 229–243.

Singer, P. (2002). *One World: The Ethics of Globalization*. New Haven, CT: Yale University Press.

Sollars, G. and Englander, F. (2007). Sweatshops: kant and consequences. *Business Ethics Quarterly* 17 (1): 113–115.

de Soto, H. (2000). *The Mystery of Capital: Why Capitalism Triumphs in the West and Fails Everywhere Else*. New York: Basic Books.

Stefanovic, M., Domeisen, N.N., and Hulm, P.P. (2007). New business-NGO partnerships help the world's poorest. *International Trade Forum* 2: 6–8.

Stout, L.A. (2012). *The Shareholder Value Myth: How Putting Shareholders First Harms Investors, Corporations, and the Public*. Berrett-Koehler Publishers.

Strudler, A. (2008). Confucian skepticism about workplace rights. *Business Ethics Quarterly* 18 (1): 67–84.

Suchman, M.C. (1995). Managing legitimacy: strategic and institutional approaches. *Academy of Management Review* 20 (3): 571–610.

Sunstein, C.R. (2003). Beyond the precautionary principle. *University of Pennsylvania Law Review* 151 (3): 1003–1058.

Tatsuo, I. (1999). Liberal democracy and Asian orientalism. In: *The East Asian Challenge for Human Rights* (ed. J.R. Bauer and D.A. Bell), 27–59. Cambridge: Cambridge University Press.

Tenbrunsel, A.E., Smith-Crowe, K., and Umphress, E.E. (2003). Building Houses on Rocks: The Role of the Ethical Infrastructure in Organizations. *Social Justice Research* 16 (3): 285–307.

The World Bank (2011). *World Development Indicators*. The World Bank.

Thompson, J.J. (1993). *The Realm of Rights*. Harvard University Press.

Tietenberg and Lewis (2008). *Environmental & Natural Resource Economics*, 8e. Pearson.

Transparency International (2015). Mission and history. http://www.transparency-usa.org/archive/who/mission.html (accessed 17 October 2015).

Treviño, L.K. and Nelson, K.A. (2010). *Managing Business Ethics*. New York: Wiley.

Unger, P. (1996). *Living High and Letting Die: Our Illusion of Innocence*. Oxford University Press.

United Nations (1966). International Covenant on Economic, Social and Cultural Rights. A/RES/21/2200. December, 16.

United Nations (2003). Commission on Human Rights, Sub-Commission on Protection & Promotion of Human Rights, Working Group. Norms on the Responsibilities of Transnational Corporations and Other Business Enterprises with Regard to Human Rights. United Nations, Doc. E/CN.4/Sub,2/2003/12/ Rev.2 (2003).

United Nations (2005). Commission on Human Rights. Human Rights Resolution 2005/69: Human Rights and Transnational Corporations and Other Business Enterprises, E/CN.4/RES/2005/69 (April 20, 2005).

United Nations (2006). Special Representative of the Secretary General on the Issue of Human Rights and Transnational Corporations and Other Business Enterprises. "Promotion and Protection of Human Rights." United Nations Doc. E/CN.4/2006/97 (February 22, 2006).

United Nations (2008). *Global Compact Office, Corporate Citizenship in the World Economy: United Nations Global Compact.* New York: United Nations.

United Nations (2008). Special Representative of the Secretary General on the Issue of Human Rights and Transnational Corporations and Other Business Enterprises."Protect, Respect and Remedy: a Framework for Business and Human Rights." United Nations Doc. A/HRC/8/5 (April 7, 2008).

United Nations Development Programme (2010). *Human Development Report: The Real Wealth of Nations: Pathways to Human Development.* New York: United Nations Development Programme (UNDP).

United Nations Special Representative of the Secretary General on the Issue of Human Rights and Transnational Corporations and Other Business Enterprises. (2006). Promotion and Protection of Human Rights. United Nations Doc. E/CN.4/2006/97 (February 22).

United Nations Special Representative of the Secretary General on the Issue of Human Rights and Transnational Corporations and Other Business Enterprises (2008). Protect, Respect and Remedy: A Framework for Business and Human Rights. United Nations Doc. A/HRC/8/5 (April 7).

United States Council for International Business (n.d.) Submission to the High Commissioner for Human Rights for the report on the Responsibilities of Transnational Corporations and Related Business Enterprises with Regard to Human Rights. Undated.

Varley, P. (ed.) (1998). *The Sweatshop Quandary: Corporate Responsibility on the Global Frontier.* New York: Investor Responsibility Research Center.

Vogel, D. (2006). *The Market for Virtue.* Washington, DC: Brookings Institute Press.

Wackernagel, M., Schulz, N.B., Deumling, D. et al. (2002). Tracking the ecological overshoot of the human economy. *Proceedings of the National Academy of Sciences* 99: 9266–9271.

Webb, J.W., Kistruck, G.M., Ireland, R., and Ketchen, J.J. (2009). The entrepreneurship process in base of the pyramid markets: the case of multinational enterprise/nongovernment organization alliances. *Entrepreneurship: Theory & Practice* 34 (3): 555–581.

Weidner, K.L., Rosa, J., and Viswanathan, M. (2010). Marketing to subsistence consumers: lessons from practice. *Journal of Business Research* 63 (6): 559–569.

Weissbrodt, D. and Kruger, M. (2003). Norms on the responsibilities of transnational corporations and other business enterprises with regard to human rights. *American Journal of International Law* 97: 901–922.

Wertheimer, A. (1996). *Exploitation.* Princeton, NJ: Princeton University Press.

Wettstein, F. (2009). *Multinational Corporations and Global Justice: Human Rights Obligations of a Quasi Governmental Institution.* Stanford, CA: Stanford University Press.

Wettstein, F. (2010). For better or for worse: do corporations have a duty to promote just institutions? *Business Ethics Quarterly* 20 (2): 275–283.

Wettstein, F. (2012a). Silence as complicity: elements of a corporate duty to speak out against the violation of human rights. *Business Ethics Quarterly* 22 (1): 37–61.

Wettstein, F. (2012b). CSR and the debate on business and human rights: bridging the great divide. *Business Ethics Quarterly* 22 (4): 739–770.

Whelan, G. (2012). The political perspective of corporate responsibility: a critical research agenda. *Business Ethics Quarterly* 22 (4): 709–737.

Williamson, O.E. (1985). *The Economic Institutions of Capitalism*. New York: Free Press.

Wilson, J.Q. (1981). Democracy and the corporation. In: *Does Big Business Rule America?* (ed. R. Hessen). Washington, DC: Ethics and Public Policy Center.

Windsor, D. (2006). Corporate social responsibility: three key approaches. *Journal of Management Studies* 43: 93–114.

Wood, A.W. (1995). Exploitation. *Social Philosophy and Policy* 12: 136–158.

Wood, A.W. (2004). *Karl Marx*, 2e. New York: Routledge.

World Business Council for Sustainable Development (2004). *SC Johnson: Pyrethrum Sourcing from Kenya*. Geneva, CH: World Business Council for Sustainable Development.

World Commission on Environment and Development (1987). *Our Common Future*. New York: Oxford University Press.

World Wildlife Fund (2010). Living Planet Report 2010: Biodiversity, biocapacity and development. Obtained through the Internet. http://www.footprintnetwork.org/press/LPR2010.pdf (accessed 14 June 2011).

Worrell, E., Price, L., Martin, N. et al. (2001). Carbon dioxide emissions from the global cement industry. *Annual Review of Energy and the Environment* 26: 303–329.

Yang, X. and Rivers, C. (2009). Antecedents of CSR practices in MNCs' subsidiaries: a stakeholder and institutional perspective. *Journal of Business Ethics* 86 (2): 155–169.

Young, I.M. (2004). Responsibility and global labor justice. *Journal of Political Philosophy* 12 (4): 365–388.

Young, I.M. (2006). Responsibility and global justice: a social connection model. *Journal of Social Philosophy* 23 (1): 102–130.

Zahra, S.A., Gedajlovic, E., Neubaum, D.O., and Shulman, J.M. (2009). A typology of social entrepreneurs: motives search processes and ethical challenges. *Journal of Business Venturing* 24: 519–532.

Zimmerman, M.J. (1996). *The Concept of Moral Obligation*. Cambridge University Press.

Zwolinski, M. (2007). Sweatshops, choice, and exploitation. *Business Ethics Quarterly* 17 (4): 689–727.

Index

Note: Page numbers with 'n' refer to notes.

The Ethics of Global Business, First Edition. Denis G. Arnold.
© 2023 John Wiley & Sons Ltd. Published 2023 by John Wiley & Sons Ltd.